Model Essays for IB and A Level Economics

GLOBAL ECONOMY Volume 2

Kelvin Hong

Shachah Chua

First Printing: 2024

ISBN 978-981-18-9966-9

Edventures Pte Ltd

Singapore

www.TheEconomicsTutor.com

PREFACE

This book answers 20 key examination questions across the entire Global Economy syllabus, which encompasses both International Trade and Development, and was created to provide students with the ability to excel in their examinations.

Very often, students are unable to provide step-by-step explanations and relevant evaluation points, which are essential to scoring in examinations.

By studying through the model essays provided in this book, students will be able to better understand the various economic concepts covered in the Global Economy syllabus. The powerful diagrammatic analyses provided will also train students to illustrate economic concepts logically, and enable them to use such diagrams for analyses in a more effective and concise manner.

The questions are mostly adapted from past IB examination papers. However, they are also very applicable to the A Level examinations.

We hope that students will now see great hope in scoring very well for their essay papers.

Kelvin Hong & Shachah Chua

Table of Contents

1. Explain how administrative barriers to trade work. (10)

Introduction

1. Administrative barriers are a form of "hidden" protectionism involving bureaucratic procedures, which governments may impose to prevent the free flow of imports into the country.

2. Oftentimes, governments may seek to justify these administrative barriers on health or safety grounds.

3. Such administrative barriers make it time-consuming and more costly for firms to import goods, therefore leading to a reduction in imports.

Bureaucratic red-tape

1. "Red-tape" are administrative processes that have to be undertaken when goods are being imported into a country. Such "red-tape" is usually lengthy and complicated, thus slowing down the flow of imports.

2. For example, importers may face complicated paperwork which causes delays in importing the goods into the country. If such paperwork also requires legal work, this delays the import process even further, raising administrative costs for the importer.

3. Countries may also limit the number of ports of entry which may be more difficult to reach and more expensive to pass through. Forcing all imports to pass through limited ports of entry also creates bottlenecks, slowing down the flow of imports further and adding more costs for importers.

4. Excessive "red-tape" is usually protectionist in nature. For example, to support its "Make in India" initiative, in 2023, India required companies like Apple, Dell, and Samsung to obtain import licences for laptops and tablets to encourage them to set up production in India instead.

Health, Safety, and Environmental Standards

1. Various restrictions can be placed on the types and quantities of imports, regulating what can be sold on the domestic market to prevent adverse health or safety effects on the population.

2. For example, although Australia has a free trade agreement with the US (AUSFTA), Australia enforces quarantine measures on agricultural imports very seriously in the name of biosecurity, and US exporters must comply with its strict regulations. This increases costs and may even result in the agricultural goods turning bad, in reality making trade infeasible.

2. Explain two methods a central bank may use to devalue a currency. (10)

Introduction

1. Devaluation refers to the deliberate decrease in the value of a currency in a fixed (or managed) exchange rate system.

2. Central banks can devalue the domestic currency by 1) buying foreign currencies, and 2) lowering interest rates.

Method 1: Foreign exchange intervention

1. In a fixed or managed exchange rate system, central banks may buy foreign currencies to devalue the currency.

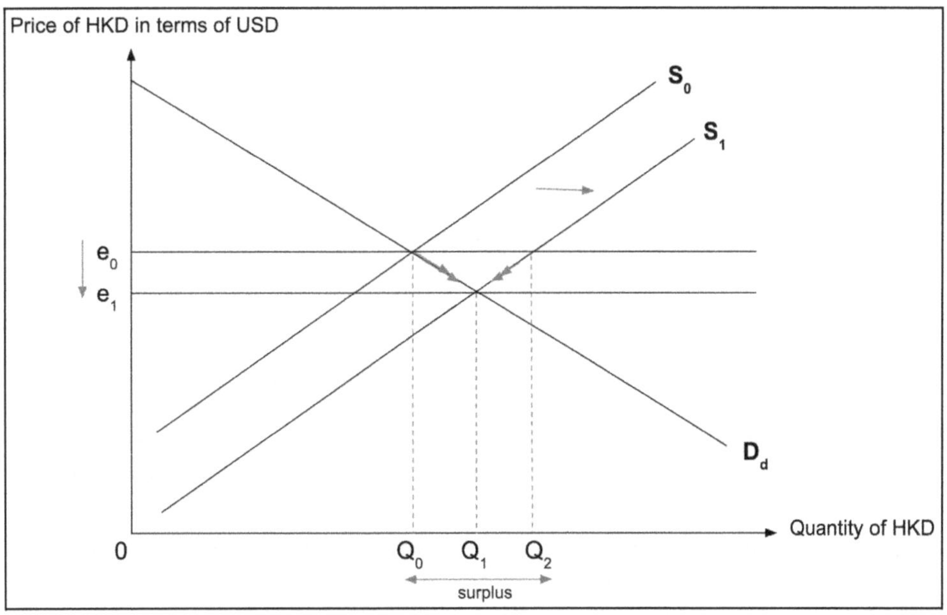

Fig 1: devaluation of HKD against USD

2. For example, if Hong Kong wishes to devalue the Hong Kong Dollar's (HKD) peg with the US dollar (USD) from e_0 to e_1, the central bank could buy more USD on the foreign exchange market, simultaneously selling HKD.

3. This increases the supply of HKD in the foreign exchange market from S_0 to S_1, and assuming constant demand for HKD, a surplus of Q_0Q_2 is created at the

original peg e_0.

4. This then places downward pressure on the equilibrium exchange rate, causing the HKD to depreciate from e_0 to e_1 against the USD.

5. The central bank can then begin to maintain the HKD's peg at the new, lower value e_1.

Method 2: Lowering interest rates

1. A central bank could also attempt to devalue its currency by lowering its interest rates.

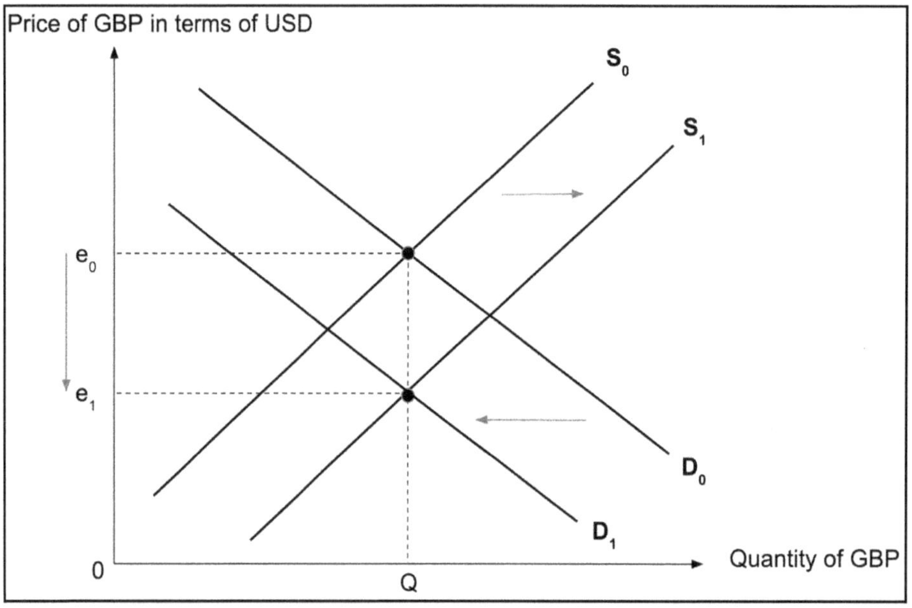

Fig 2: effect of lowering interest rates on exchange rate

2. Lowered interest rates makes it less attractive for hot money investors to save in the domestic country due to lower returns. Thus, hot money investors will likely withdraw funds from the country and this would increase outflow of financial capital.

3. These investors would sell more domestic currency to buy foreign currency, increasing the supply of domestic currency in the foreign exchange market from S_0 to S_1, causing the supply curve to shift rightwards.

4. For the same reason, there would be a fall in hot money inflows, reducing the demand for the domestic currency from D_0 to D_1 and causing the demand

curve to shift leftwards.

5. The shifts in the demand and supply curves will reinforce each other in causing a devaluation of the domestic currency from e_0 to e_1.

3. Using real world examples, evaluate the implications of a current account surplus. (15)

Introduction

1. The current account (CA) is one of three accounts in a country's Balance of Payments (BOP), and is the sum of the Balance of Trade (BOT) or net export revenue, net income flows and net current transfers.

2. A surplus in the current account means that the value of the current account balance is positive and the total inflows exceed total outflows

3. Since the BOT is usually the largest component of the CA, a CA surplus is usually caused by a trade surplus, which is when export revenue (X) exceeds import expenditure (M) for currently produced goods & services.

Positive 1: CA surplus is indicative of strong economic growth

1. In export-driven economies, a strong CA surplus can be indicative of strong economic growth. High export revenues (X) relative to import expenditure (M) not only creates large BOT and CA surpluses but also likely increases aggregate demand (AD), since net exports (X–M) is a component of AD.

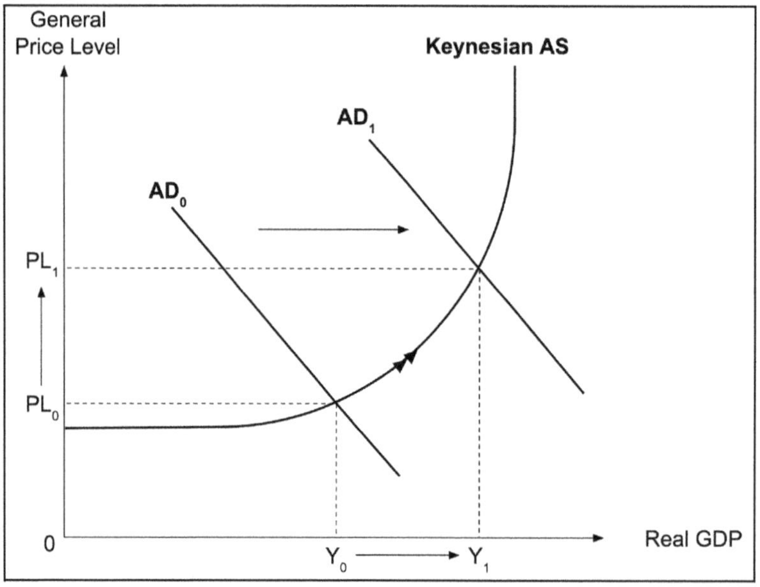

Fig 1: real GDP growth from higher net exports (X–M)

2. The AD curve shift rightwards from AD_0 to AD_1. Real GDP, determined from where the AD curve intersects the Keynesian Aggregate Supply (AS) curve, thus increases from Y_0 to Y_1, indicating actual economic growth.

3. The increase in real output implies higher derived demand for labour as firms increase output by employing more resources. Unemployment thus falls as more workers are hired.

4. With economic growth and a fall in unemployment, per capita income is likely to increase assuming the population remains fairly stable, thus the average person can enjoy more goods and services, leading to higher material standards of living.

5. China's export-driven growth as "the world's factory" led to its real GDP increasing from US$3 trillion in 2001 to US$6.24 trillion in 2008. Over the same period, its CA surplus increased dramatically from US$17.4 billion to US$420.57 billion.

6. Employment in export-led sectors like manufacturing increased, and many rural workers in China migrated to urban areas to take up such employment. China's GNI per capita (PPP) also increased from US$3,160 in 2001 to US$7,630 in 2008.

Positive 2: Funds for foreign investment

1. With a CA surplus, the country is earning foreign exchange, which can then be spent to acquire overseas assets in the form of portfolio and direct investments, or loans to other countries; it could also be treated as additions to a country's foreign reserves.

2. China's aforementioned increase in their CA surplus was also met with a massive increase in its foreign reserves, from US$220.06 billion in 2001 to US$1.97 trillion in 2008. This led to the establishment of the China Investment Corporation (CIC) in 2007, the country's largest sovereign wealth fund today, which would use the reserves to invest (both portfolio and FDI) abroad and generate returns which would benefit the country.

3. Through investing in overseas sectors such as oil, gas and mining, the CIC's returns on investment then counts as inflows of income under the CA and further increases the CA surplus. This also helps to increase China's real national income, seen through China's real GNI increasing from US$3.56 trillion in 2007 to US$14.57 trillion in 2020.

4. In 2015, the CIC also established a subsidiary, CIC Capital, to utilise China's large foreign reserves to support its Belt and Road Initiative (BRI). In doing so, the foreign reserves accumulated from China's CA surplus is then loaned out to developing countries for BRI projects, such as infrastructure.

5. Developing countries benefit as the BRI loan funds can then fill the savings-investment gap, being used for investments in infrastructure which promote growth and development. For example, the Standard Gauge Railway in Kenya was funded by such loan funds and was estimated to have boosted Kenya's real GDP by 1.5%.

6. Chinese firms also benefit as the BRI projects then create new markets for them to expand their operations into. For example, Chinese construction companies can be contracted to build infrastructure in developing countries while also providing the technological know-how, as was the case with Indonesia's high-speed railway.

<u>Positive 3: Currency appreciation makes imports cheaper; disinflation</u>

1. CA surpluses will create an upward pressure on the value of a country's currency. This is because the net inflows of foreign exchange leads to an excess demand for the domestic currency.

2. The quantity demanded (Q_d) of the currency then exceeds the quantity supplied (Q_s) in the foreign exchange market at the original exchange rate e_0, creating a shortage.

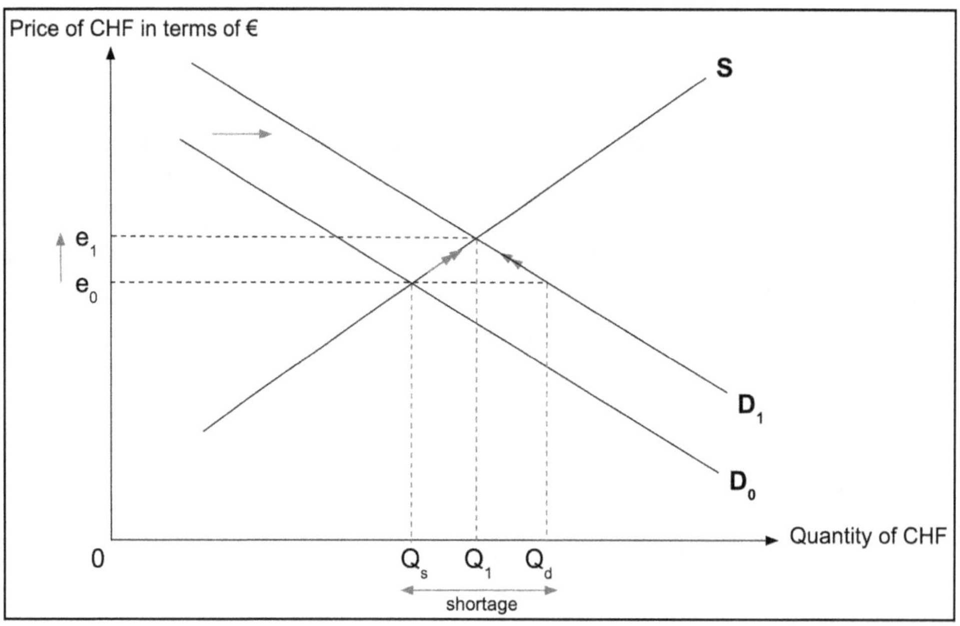

Fig 2: upward pressure on CHF due to CA surplus

3. The shortage then causes the currency to appreciate to the new exchange rate e_1, where $Q_s = Q_d$ and the shortage is eliminated.

4. As shown in Fig 2, this was the case with the Swiss franc (CHF) appreciating against the euro from CHF 1 = €0.60 in January 2008 to CHF 1 = €0.80 in January 2011, as a result of Switzerland's CA surplus from strong exports.

5. The appreciation then made imports cheaper since CHF 1 can then buy more euros and other foreign currencies. This reduces the costs to import physical capital and other raw materials. For example, 40% of construction companies in Switzerland reported "positive effects" on business activity, with 70% reporting "lower input costs" thanks to the appreciation.

6. As shown in Fig 3 below, firms can then increase their output at any price level since unit costs are reduced, causing the Short-run Aggregate Supply to increase from $SRAS_0$ to $SRAS_1$.

7. The general price level, determined from where the Aggregate Demand (AD) curve intersects the SRAS curve, then falls from PL_0 to PL_1.

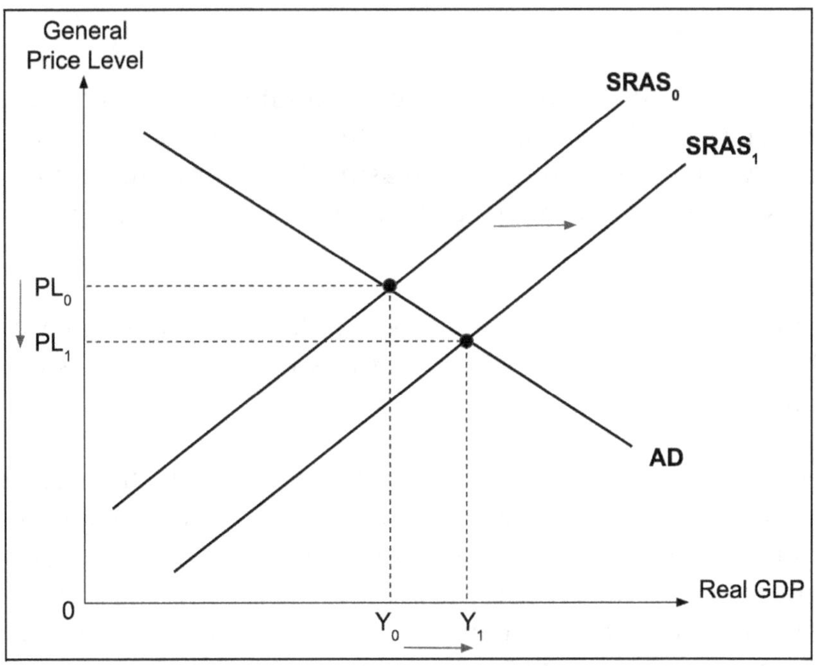

Fig 3: effect of CHF appreciation on price levels

8. This represents an easing of inflationary pressures as a result of the appreciation of the CHF. From 2008 to 2011, Switzerland's CPI only increased 0.40%, whereas the neighbouring EU's Harmonised Index of Consumer Prices (HICP) increased 4.51%.

9. Consumers in Switzerland thus experienced higher material welfare as both necessities and luxuries become relatively cheaper, and costs of living do not increase as much compared to in the EU.

<u>Negative 1: Currency appreciation makes export sectors less competitive</u>

1. However, with the same CHF appreciation, more euros or other currencies are then needed to buy CHF 1, making Swiss-made goods & services more expensive for foreigners.

2. While Switzerland's CA surplus was created from strong exports, such as in pharmaceuticals and watches, the corresponding CHF appreciation would cause these sectors to become less competitive, which then causes them to decline as the demand for these exports decreases.

3. 51% of manufacturing companies (including pharmaceuticals & watch-making) reported "significantly negative effects" from the CHF appreciation, and over 60% reported "lower profit margins" from foreign sales.

4. In response to the lower export profitability, firms may choose to cut labour costs. Close to 15% of "negatively affected" companies reported cutting labour costs by "reducing staff", increasing structural unemployment in export sectors. Around 7% also chose to cut labour costs by "cutting wages / compensation".

5. Overall, workers in these sectors would thus experience a dip in material welfare as some are laid off and others have their wages cut, lowering their incomes.

6. There is also a phenomenon known as the Dutch disease. This happened in the 1960s in the Netherlands when it discovered major natural gas fields leading to huge exports of these resources. Whilst she enjoyed current account surpluses, the appreciation of its currency led to a loss of price competitiveness for the manufacturing sector, which subsequently contracted, hurting economic growth and employment.

Negative 2: Retaliation by other countries

1. Given the nature of trade, having a large CA surplus usually corresponds to large CA deficits in other countries. This can lead to deficit countries imposing trade restrictions so as to reduce the CA deficit.

2. For example, the US has historically imported more from China than it has exported, and in 2017, had a US$375.6 billion trade deficit (2017) with China. In the same year the US CA deficit stood at US$367.61 billion.

3. In 2018, under Trump, the US imposed tariffs of US$50 billion on Chinese goods, to which China responded days later by imposing tariffs on 128 US products.

4. The tit-for-tat retaliatory trade restrictions escalated to a trade war, from which neither country benefited. For the US, manufacturers faced higher import costs and a net loss of manufacturing jobs, while consumers faced higher prices. China faced lower industrial output growth and slower economic growth amidst a fall in exports and a loss of FDI. The impacts of the trade war is still hurting the Chinese economy even in 2024.

5. Thus, having large CA surplus may be regarded as an unbalanced trading relationship and can lead to detrimental consequences for both trading partners and the surplus country.

Negative 3: CA surplus could also be indicative of low consumption

1. While a CA surplus could be attributed to strong exports, it could also be attributed to having low consumption and low import expenditure, as is the case with Japan's CA surplus post-1990s to 2000s.

2. Japan's recession in the early 1990s led to lower incomes earned by workers, reducing their purchasing power and their ability to drive consumption of goods & services, including imports. Together with deflation and lack of consumer confidence, consumption and import expenditure (M) fell, leading to Japan's improvement in the BOT, resulting in a CA surplus.

3. Thus, in such a case, the CA surplus is indicative of a low material standard of living.

Concluding Section

1. Although CA surpluses tend to be looked at favourably for its potential to boost economic growth and increase ownership of foreign assets, it is not

necessary that economies will benefit from having a CA surplus.

2. The larger and more persistent the CA surplus is, the more problematic it may be. Besides sparking off a trade war, this also includes driving up inflation as the AD may be increasing in excess of the Aggregate Supply (AS).

3. It also depends on the causes of the CA surplus. If it is due to increased exports competitiveness and higher foreign incomes, then it will more likely lead to positive effects for the economy.

4. Using real world examples, discuss the relative advantages and disadvantages of a freely floating exchange rate system, in contrast with a fixed exchange rate system. (15)

Introduction

1. The exchange rate is the price of one currency in terms of another.

2. A freely floating exchange rate system is one where the exchange rate of a currency is entirely determined by market forces of supply and demand for the currency.

3. A fixed exchange rate system is one where the exchange rate of a currency is pegged at a certain value, often in terms of US dollars (US$), by the central bank of a country, and is not allowed to fluctuate in accordance to market forces of supply and demand for the currency.

Advantage 1: Trade deficits can be self-correcting under free float

1. The balance of trade (BOT) is usually the largest component of the current account (CA), thus trade deficits generally lead to current account deficits.

2. Trade deficits ($X_{rev} - M_{exp} < 0$) occur when the import expenditure (M) exceeds export revenue (X) from currently produced goods & services.

3. In 2022, Japan recorded a record annual trade deficit of US$155 billion after prices for fuel imports, which Japan is heavily reliant on, dramatically increased, causing import expenditure (M) to grow much larger than export revenue (X).

4. This is especially since fuel is a necessity and so its demand is price-inelastic. An increase in the price of fuel would then lead to a less than proportionate decrease in quantity demanded, increasing import expenditure.

5. More yen is sold to buy more foreign currency in order to pay for the more expensive imported fuel. This leads to the supply of yen available for exchange increasing from S_0 to S_1. The equilibrium exchange rate, determined from where the supply curve (S) intersects the demand curve (D) for yen, falls from e_0 to e_1 as a result (Fig 1), showing how the trade deficit resulted in the

yen's depreciation.

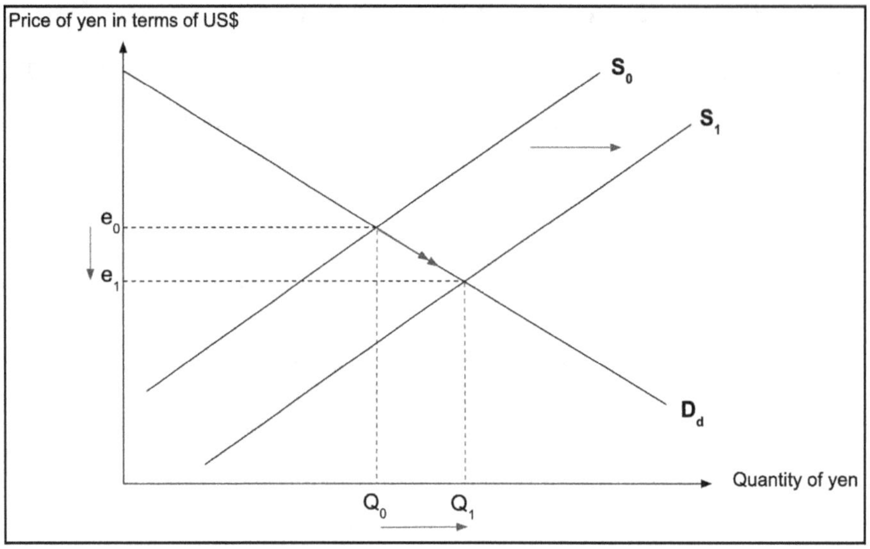

Fig 1: yen depreciation from trade deficit

6. However, the cheaper yen means that one unit of foreign currency can buy more units of yen, making Japanese exports cheaper for foreigners. This benefits Japanese exported goods as they become more competitive, and the demand for these exports increases, leading to export revenues (X) increasing.

7. At the same time, since one unit of yen can now buy less foreign currency, imports become more expensive, leading to the quantity demanded for imports decreasing. This will lead to import expenditure (M) decreasing, assuming $PED_m > 1$.

8. As long as the Marshall-Lerner condition is satisfied ($PED_m + PED_x > 1$), then the BOT ($X_{rev} - M_{exp}$) improves and the trade deficit shrinks, ceteris paribus; by extension, this also leads to the CA deficit shrinking.

9. In June 2023, Japan's BOT actually recovered to a surplus (its first in 2 years) of US$308 million thanks to increased exports of cars and construction machinery, as a result of them becoming cheaper from the depreciating yen.

10. A fixed exchange rate system lacks this self-correction mechanism since the central bank would not allow the price of the currency to fall, instead intervening by selling its reserves and buying back the domestic currency, increasing the demand for the currency and maintaining the fixed rate.

Advantage 2: Free floats allow for monetary policy flexibility

1. Floating exchange rate systems give policymakers greater flexibility in using monetary policy and interest rates as a tool to influence the domestic economy. This is unlike in fixed exchange rate systems, where monetary policy must be in line with supporting the currency peg.

2. For example, if its currency's value is facing downward pressure, such as due to surplus in the foreign exchange market, the central bank may have to increase interest rates, as this can help attract hot money inflows from foreign investors due to greater returns.

3. As shown in Fig 2 below, this increases the demand for the domestic currency (from D_0 to D_1) as more foreign currency is being sold to buy domestic currency for these investments.

4. Since the equilibrium exchange rate is determined from where the demand curve (D) intersects the supply curve (S), the increase in demand causes the price of the domestic currency to increase from e_0 to the fixed rate e_{fixed}.

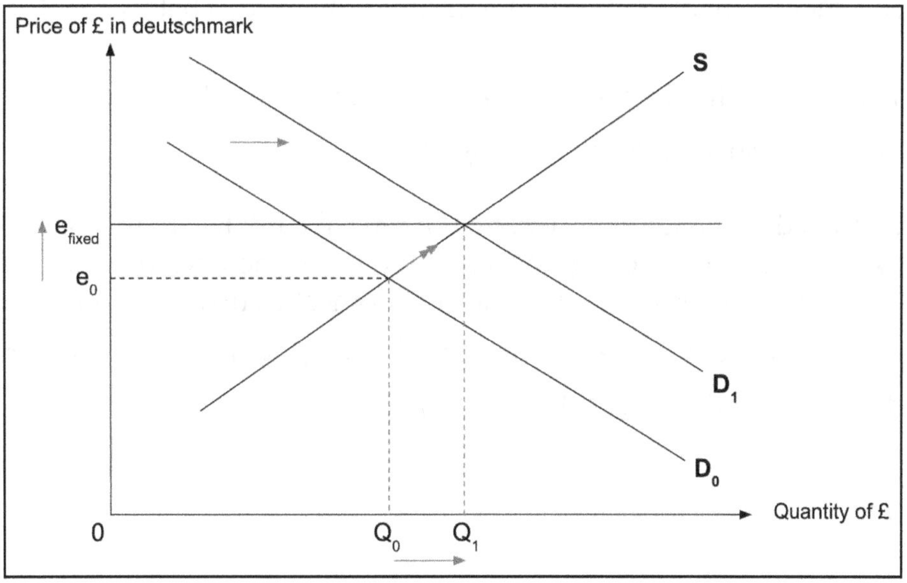

Fig 2: increasing interest rates to maintain currency peg

5. However, increasing interest rates has contractionary effects on the domestic economy. It increases the cost of borrowing for consumers to finance big ticket items, and for firms to finance investment projects, therefore reducing consumption (C) and investment (I); since these are components of aggregate demand (AD) and real GDP, a slowdown of economic growth occurs.

6. In September 1992, to prevent the pound (£) from falling too far below the European Exchange Rate Mechanism (ERM) band's lower limit (e_{fixed} in Fig 2 above), the UK government increased the base interest rate from the already very high 10% to 12% to increase demand for the pound.

7. At that time, the UK was in a recession and unemployment had hit 3 million, but due to its commitment to the ERM, it lost the ability to use monetary policy to stimulate growth. The high interest rates only made mortgage payments more expensive, leading to homeowners having lower disposable incomes, causing lower C and AD.

8. Central banks in countries with floating exchange rates do not face this need to increase interest rates to defend its currency while risking contractionary effects.

<u>Advantage 3: Free floats do not deplete foreign reserves, and face less risk from speculative attacks</u>

1. Speculation can lead to the value of a currency falling as speculators begin to sell holdings of the domestic currency, increasing the supply of domestic currency available for exchange from S_0 to S_1 (Fig 3 below).

2. This causes the domestic currency to depreciate (Fig 3 below: e_{fixed} to e_1), as discussed earlier (*under Advantage 1*).

3. In a fixed exchange rate system, the central bank has to intervene by selling off foreign reserves and buying back the domestic currency. As shown in Fig 3 below, this increases demand for the domestic currency from D_0 to D_1, causing the equilibrium price to increase from e_1 back to the fixed rate e_{fixed}, as discussed earlier (*under Advantage 2*).

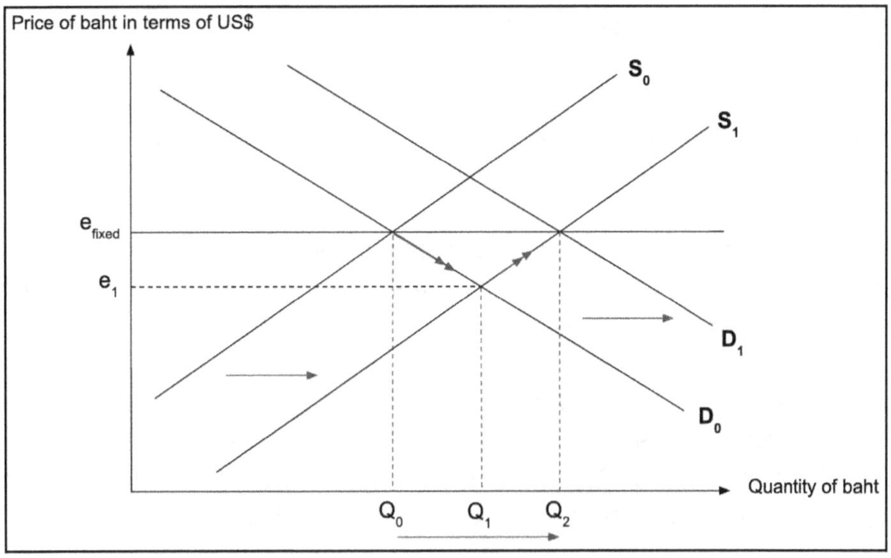

Fig 3: defending a currency peg in a fixed regime

4. However, this method of defending the fixed exchange rate using foreign reserves becomes unsustainable in the long run, especially if the central bank does not hold enough foreign reserves.

5. In the 1997 Asian Financial Crisis, Thailand and Indonesia faced speculative attacks as investors lost confidence in the respective countries' currencies and their central banks' abilities to defend them.

6. Thailand had pegged the baht to the US dollar while Indonesia managed the rupiah within a trading band. Both exhausted their foreign reserves trying to control their currency values.

7. Eventually, both were forced to float their currencies, leading to sharp depreciations as they had been overvalued. Many firms in both countries defaulted as they became unable to cope with the increased costs of serving debts denominated in foreign currencies, leading to higher unemployment and poverty.

8. As floating exchange rates are determined by market forces of demand and supply, and automatically adjust to changes in economic conditions (such as trade deficits as aforementioned), central banks are not obligated to hold large foreign reserves just to deplete them and defend their overvalued currencies.

9. It is also more difficult for currency traders to "attack" a floating currency and force a sharp devaluation.

Disadvantage 1: Free floats can lead to worsened imported inflation

1. Floating exchange rate systems could contribute to imported inflation, especially if the country is reliant on its imports, such as for necessities like food and fuel, as well as for capital goods.

2. In a free float, if a country's currency experiences depreciation, then one unit of the domestic currency can buy less foreign currency, making foreign goods and services more expensive.

3. Since capital goods and other inputs become more expensive for firms to import, this increases their costs of production so less output can be produced at any price level. As shown in Fig 4 below, this leads to the short-run aggregate supply decreasing from $SRAS_0$ to $SRAS_1$.

4. Since the general price level is determined from where the SRAS curve intersects the AD curve, the general price level increases from PL_0 to PL_1.

5. Furthermore, the decrease in real GDP from Y_0 to Y_1 represents a contraction in the economy.

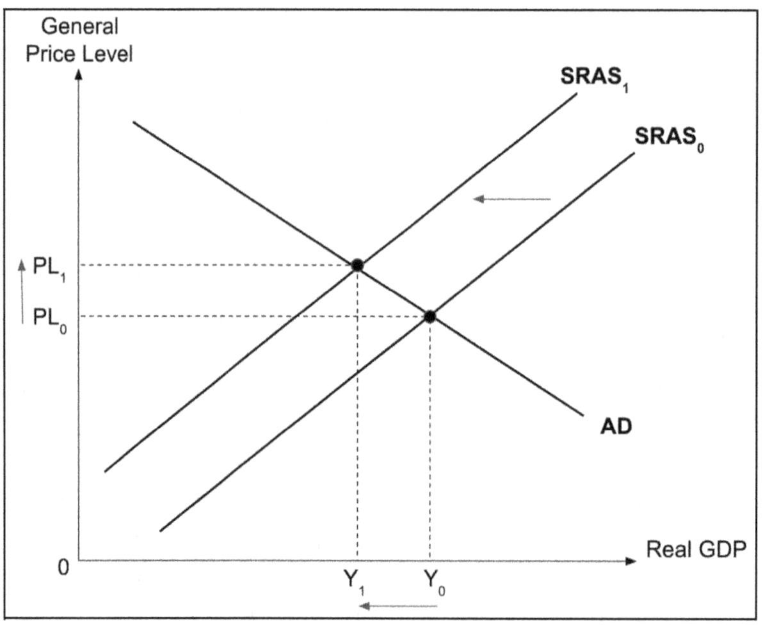

Fig 4: imported inflation from currency depreciation

6. This increase in the general price level is the inflation caused by the depreciation of the currency, which could worsen already existing inflationary

pressures from overseas supply shocks increasing import costs.

7. Consumers will as a result have to face higher costs of living and worsened material standard of living as their purchasing power falls; unemployment also increases as less output is produced and firms offset costs by laying off workers.

8. In 2018-19, the Turkish lira experienced sharp depreciations, which caused imported food, fuels, and capital goods to become more expensive. This contributed to record-high inflation which left ⅔ of people unable to afford food and rent, together with causing unemployment to soar from 10.9% to 13.9%.

9. In such situations, fixed exchange rates could have prevented the inflationary pressures.

Disadvantage 2: Free floats are subject to volatility / fixed exchange rates offer greater certainty

1. Floating exchange rates are subject to greater volatility as any abrupt changes to the demand or supply of the domestic currency leads to abrupt changes in the exchange rate.

2. This causes producers greater uncertainty as they become less able to plan accurately for the future, given that costs to import or export both consumer goods and factors of production will fluctuate and be unpredictable. Furthermore, inward investment flows become limited as foreign investors have less confidence in the value of their returns in the future.

3. On the other hand, fixed exchange rates, with their higher degree of certainty, could promote greater economic growth and trade. Firms can better plan future investments, with greater certainty on export revenue from goods sold and costs of imported inputs.

4. With more FDI inflows increasing investments (I), this then increases AD, boosting real GDP growth.

5. For example, China's export-led growth was made possible greatly due to its undervalued currency peg, especially from 1994 to 2005. Chinese producers had confidence that the central bank would maintain the very undervalued peg, and could easily plan their export revenues, allocating resources towards producing export goods to maximise profits. FDI inflows into China also increased. These helped China's real GDP grow from US$564 billion in 1994 to

US$2 trillion in 2005.

6. A fixed exchange rate can also instil discipline in domestic producers as they cannot rely on depreciation to become more competitive, for both their exports which become cheaper, and against imports which become more expensive. This encourages firms to increase productive efficiency by lowering input costs, which would not only keep price levels low for consumers (and curb inflation), but also encourage R&D which would improve productivity and increase the economy's potential output, leading to potential economic growth.

7. Between 1991 and 2002, Argentina pegged the peso to the US dollar at one-to-one parity. By pegging against a strong currency, Argentinian producers could not depend on a weakening peso to boost export competitiveness. Firms then invested in more productive, capital-intensive technologies which replaced labour and lowered labour costs, helping them maintain profitability and competitiveness. Inflation was then tamed and real GDP growth was sustained at an average of 4.7% annually.

<u>Disadvantage 3: Floating exchange rates are also susceptible to speculation which could be destabilising too</u>

1. If investors and currency traders lose confidence in a currency and speculate its value to fall, they will sell off their holdings of the domestic currency which leads to the domestic currency depreciating, as discussed earlier (*under Advantage 3*).

2. The falling value of the currency can lead to further loss of confidence and greater speculation, which could cause even greater depreciation, fueling a self-fulfilling cycle which could cause a currency's value to free-fall.

3. This could cause significant imported inflation and worsen material welfare, as discussed earlier (*under Disadvantage 1*).

4. In 2014, prices of crude oil (a major export of Russia) fell by 50% and Russia was hit by international sanctions. Many investors lost confidence in the Russian economy and sold off its Russian assets.

5. This created a significant outflow of financial capital and a rapid increase in the supply of Ruble in the foreign exchange market. The value of the Ruble subsequently fell from 36.25 per USD (Mar 2014) to 68.49 per USD (Dec 2014) before the central bank intervened.

6. The sharp depreciation of the Ruble led to sharp inflation, as prices of imported goods like beef and fish rose 40-50%.

7. Fixed exchange rates can help insulate consumers from the effects of speculation and loss of confidence, as central banks would have to intervene to defend the fixed rate.

8. During the 1997 Asian Financial Crisis, the Hong Kong Monetary Authority (HKMA), which is the central bank, defended the Hong Kong dollar's peg to the US dollar from speculative, downward pressures by spending US$10 billion from its foreign reserves. Compared to other Asian nations affected by the crisis, consumers in Hong Kong were relatively less affected due to the HKMA's intervention.

Concluding Section

1. Both free floating and fixed exchange rates bring about their own advantages, owing to their nature of being market-driven and stable respectively.

2. Ultimately, whether one system is more beneficial to a country than the other is dependent on the country itself.

3. For example, fixed exchange rates may be better for developing nations since the stability helps promote financial inflows and more efficient producers, as well as controlling inflation.

4. On the other hand, floating exchange rates may be better for countries without large foreign reserves, since there is no need to continually defend the currency.

5. Many countries like Singapore now implement a managed float, where the value of a currency is allowed to float within some limits before the central bank intervenes. This hybrid system gives economies some flexibility afforded by free floats, while also providing some degree of certainty as under fixed exchange rates, thus achieving some benefits of both free floating and fixed exchange rate systems.

5. Explain the objectives and functions of the World Trade Organisation. (10)

<u>Introduction</u>

1. The World Trade Organisation (WTO) is an intergovernmental organisation which provides the institutional and legal framework for international trade.

2. It is responsible for liberalising trade, operating a system of trade rules, providing a forum for trade negotiations between governments, and for settling trade disputes.

<u>Administering international trade agreements to liberalise trade</u>

1. One of the functions of the WTO is to administer international trade agreements, so as to promote freer trade.

2. Trade agreements to reduce tariffs, quotas, and other restrictions, such as the General Agreement on Tariffs and Trade (GATT), are signed by WTO member states and then ratified.

3. Upon joining the WTO, a country "binds" their commitments, leading to ceilings on customs and tariff rates which they must adhere to, making their markets more open. If they want to change their bindings, they would have to negotiate with their trading partners, which could mean compensating them for a loss of trade.

4. 80% of WTO members had a drop in country-specific ad-valorem tariffs upon joining, and members experienced an increase in aggregate trade by 35% on average.

<u>Forum for trade negotiations & settlement of trade disputes</u>

1. An important function of the WTO is that it acts as a forum for trade negotiations.

2. The highest institutional body within the WTO is the Ministerial Conference (MC), which meets every two years. All members are brought together at the MC, at which decisions regarding any matters under any of the WTO's multilateral trade agreements are made.

3. For example, at MC9 in Bali (2013), 159 members of the WTO successfully negotiated and agreed on the Bali Package, which were a set of decisions to lower import tariffs, and for developed countries to lower agricultural subsidies and abolish import quotas for agricultural products from developing countries.

4. The WTO also handles trade disputes through its Dispute Settlement Body (DSB), which it considers as its "unique contribution" to the global economy. The DSB helps promote stability while making international trade an enforceable rules-based system.

5. Disputes occur when a country believes another country has violated trade rules. Instead of taking action unilaterally, WTO members could go through the DSB and abide by agreed procedures.

6. The DSB consists of all WTO members and is responsible for setting up panels of experts to consider each case. Once the DSB makes a ruling on the case, the offending country is given time to bring its policies into line with the ruling or recommendations.

7. If the offending country fails to act within this time period, then it must negotiate on appropriate compensation with the complaining countries.

Technical assistance and training for developing countries

1. Another function of the WTO is to assist economically least developed countries (ELDCs) in using trade as an engine for growth, as well as promoting sustainable development and poverty reduction.

2. For example, the WTO helps ELDCs build capacity to trade, which includes addressing important supply-side issues.

3. The WTO also provides country-specific analysis to help recipient countries identify priorities to guide their trade agendas, constraints to trade integration, and provide advice on key areas.

4. Based on such studies, the ELDC then implements the priority projects in the recommendations, and can seek financial assistance from the WTO's trust funds.

5. The WTO, together with other agencies (which includes IMF, World Bank, UNDP) also help to provide Trade-Related Technical Assistance (TRTA) to ELDCs to build capacity and infrastructure. Such TRTA includes providing

courses on trade policy, trade negotiations skills, and other workshops.

6. Furthermore, ELDCs could also request Aid for Trade resources from the WTO, which could help them develop the infrastructure needed for trade.

6. Explain two factors that limit the effectiveness of the World Trade Organisation in achieving its objectives. (10)

Introduction

1. The World Trade Organisation (WTO) is an intergovernmental organisation which provides the institutional and legal framework for international trade.

2. While it does claim to offer benefits to the global trading system and contribute to the development of free trade, how much the WTO actually benefits different countries globally has been subject to much criticism.

WTO promotes trade rules which do not favour developing nations

1. All agreements made within the WTO must be implemented by members, however this could lead to greater effects in certain nations than others.

2. For example, the Agreement on Trade-Related Aspects of Intellectual Property Rights (TRIPS) benefits developed countries much more compared to developing and least developed nations.

3. By protecting the intellectual property of certain technologies in developed nations, developing and least developed nations face higher costs of acquiring such technology which could be much needed to spur economic growth and development.

4. Furthermore, while the WTO has greatly reduced tariff rates globally, it has not done enough to address the use of non-tariff and hidden barriers.

5. These barriers, including supposed "anti-dumping" measures against exports by developing countries, allow developed countries to still protect certain domestic industries against goods produced by developing countries.

6. This leads to lower export revenues for developing countries, limiting the ability for these countries to use trade as an engine for growth.

7. Lowering trade barriers for all economies – rich or poor – is also not entirely beneficial for developing countries as they might need trade protection to develop their infant industries, diversifying production and reducing risk of becoming "trapped" in the primary goods sector.

The WTO has been accused of being undemocratic

1. Even though all countries are said to have an equal vote in the WTO, some economies, especially the USA and the EU as two of the largest markets in the world, are thought to have too much power in the WTO and its negotiations.

2. These larger, developed economies often dominate agenda-setting and have voices which may carry more weight. This could result in the views and aspirations of developing countries being unheard and ignored. The outcomes of the negotiations may then advantage developed economies more than developing ones.

3. Industrialised, developed economies may also hold "informal meetings" amongst themselves and behind closed doors to negotiate important decisions while completely excluding any input from developing economies. This was the case in the 1999 WTO Ministerial Conference where developing countries' representatives criticised the US and the EU for holding exclusive talks to negotiate on a mutual deal on agriculture.

4. The consensus-based decision-making within the WTO has also been criticised as undemocratic since no member present must object to the decision being made. The difficulty in reaching a consensus has led to fragmentation between members. Historically, negotiations between the US, EU, and developing economies have failed over the US and EU unwillingness to give up their agricultural subsidies, and progress on agricultural issues has been very slow.

5. Developing nations may also lack the capacity, human resources, and technical expertise to be able to follow along with the negotiations and participate actively, limiting the ability for their opinion to be heard.

7. Using real world examples, evaluate the view that market-based policies may be ineffective in promoting the economic development of the world's poorest countries. (15)

Introduction

1. Economic development is the sustained improvement in both material and non-material economic well-being of residents in a country.

2. Material well-being refers to the quantity and quality of goods & services available for consumption to consumers.

3. Non-material well-being refers to less tangible quality of life factors, such as education and health standards, environmental quality and the amount of leisure.

4. Market-based policies refer to reduction of government intervention in the economy so as to make markets more responsive to the forces of supply and demand, which may improve productive and allocative efficiency.

Thesis 1: Market-based policies give rise to market failures

(a) Merit goods

1. Market-based policies, such as privatisation of publicly-owned enterprises, can lead to the underprovision of merit goods. Such merit goods have positive consumption externalities, meaning that consumption of such goods leads to external benefits by third parties.

2. For example, in 1999-2000, the city of Cochabamba in Bolivia privatised its water supply company. Clean water is a merit good given that consuming clean water reduces workers' vulnerability to water-borne diseases, making them healthier and more productive, benefitting third parties including family members and employers. Therefore, as seen in Fig 1 below, the marginal social benefit of consuming clean water (MSB) is greater than the marginal private benefit (MPB).

3. As shown in Fig 1 below, the quantity of clean water provided for at market equilibrium (Q_{eqm}) is determined where the marginal private benefit (MPB) to

consumers equals the marginal private cost (MPC) to firms.

4. The socially optimal quantity (Q_{opt}) is determined where the marginal social benefit (MSB) equals the marginal social cost (MSC).
5. Thus, $Q_{eqm} < Q_{opt}$, which represents the free market under-allocating resources to provide clean water.

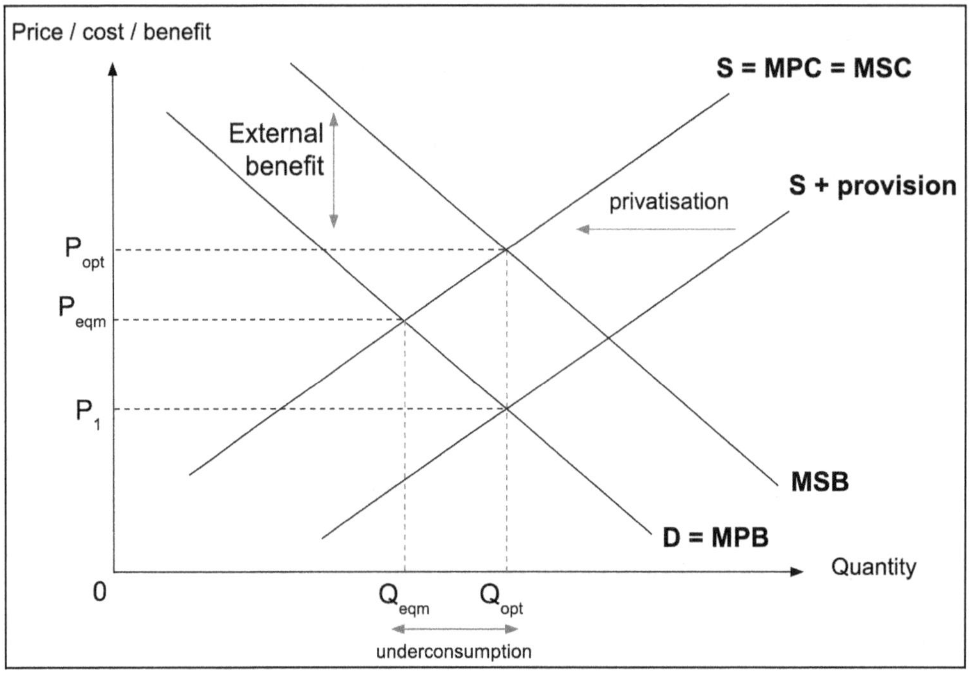

Fig 1: underprovision of clean water after privatisation

6. Previous government intervention in the form of provision would have led to greater supply ($S + provision$) of clean water and Q_{opt} being provided for in the market, at a lower price P_1. However, as the private sector is motivated to maximise profits, they may produce a lower quantity Q_{eqm} at a higher price P_{eqm}.
7. In Cochabamba, water prices increased by an average of 35%, becoming unaffordable for many residents and forcing many residents to switch to more unsafe and dirty water sources.
8. With limited access to clean water from the free market, workers are then more likely to contract water-borne diseases, limiting their human capital, resulting in low labour productivity and low incomes.

9. This traps workers in a poverty cycle (Fig 2 below) as they become less able to afford healthcare and education for themselves or their children, severely limiting both material and non-material well-being, which prevents development.

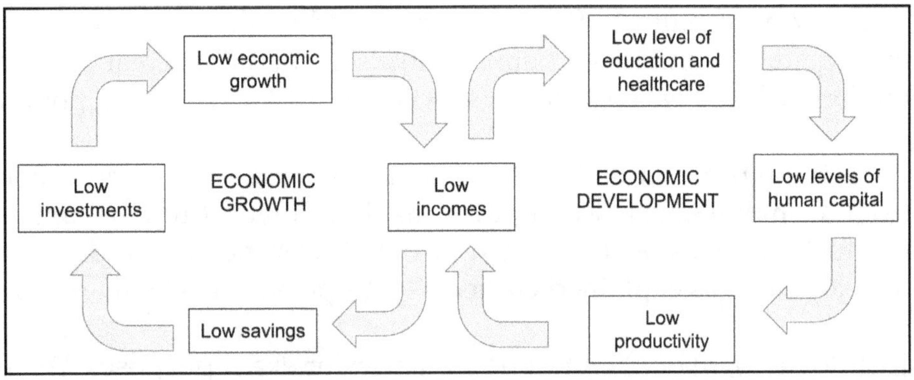

Fig 2: poverty cycle diagram

(b) Public goods

1. Profit-maximising firms are unwilling to provide public goods (which are non-rivalrous and non-excludable) since they suffer from the free-rider problem, where users can enjoy using the good without paying for it.

2. For example, in Bangladesh, private firms would not provide flood control & prevention systems (a public good).

3. Without such flood prevention systems, flooding leads to lower agricultural output and lower incomes for farmers, thus leading to lower material well-being. In Bangladesh, the coastal areas are home to 400,000 people, a higher-than-average percentage of which live in absolute poverty.

4. These farmers also become trapped in the poverty cycle (Fig 2) and become unable to afford education and healthcare, leading to lower non-material well-being.

5. With the free market unable to provide flood control systems, the Bangladesh government (with aid from the World Bank) has had to intervene to provide them and promote development for those living near the coastal areas.

(c) Negative Environmental Externalities

1. Market-oriented policies could encourage increased production of goods that generate negative production externalities.

2. In the 1980s, Ghana simplified and relaxed regulations for the gold and diamond mining sectors, as well as reduced corporate taxes. Small-scale gold mining was also legalised, meaning small firms were allowed to enter the mining sector.

3. This increased output of diamond and gold while causing clean water sources to be polluted with toxic chemicals like mercury, thus creating external costs in the form of medical costs to those who fall ill from drinking polluted water.

4. With the more polluted water, Ghanaian workers are more likely to fall ill from drinking such water, thus having lower human capital and lower productivity. This leads to them earning lower incomes and limiting economic development, as explained earlier (Fig 2 – poverty cycle diagram).

(Note: Just doing a), b) or c) would be sufficient for exam purposes. We are providing more here for your learning purposes.)

<u>Thesis 2: Market-based policies lead to greater income inequality</u>

1. In the 1980s and 1990s, Ghana underwent structural adjustment which included market-based policies like trade liberalisation and privatisation of certain sectors, such as cocoa exports.

2. Privatisation of the cocoa exports sector led to the incomes received by cocoa farmers becoming more uneven. Larger-scale cocoa farmers who owned more factors of production and were able to take advantage of economies of scale to produce at lower average costs, thus being more profitable.

3. On the other hand, smaller-scale cocoa farmers were less profitable and financially insecure. These farmers faced higher average costs and struggled to compete with other cocoa producers globally and cope with price volatility. This included farmers in very rural areas who struggled with the high costs of transporting their crops to urban areas, where markets were located.

4. 5 years into the Structural Adjustment Program, only 18% of cocoa-farming households benefited from an increase in the world price for cocoa. 32% of cocoa farmers received 94% of the gross cocoa income.

5. The private sector, including manufacturing, was also negatively affected by trade liberalisation as it struggled to cope with global competition, especially from East Asia. These foreign producers were relatively more efficient compared to Ghanaian producers, and domestic producers were incentivised to cut costs to maintain profitability.

6. Firms mainly did so by cutting labour costs, either by reducing wages or laying off workers; 48,000 jobs were lost in the private sector due to foreign competition. This led to reduced incomes for many workers.

7. All these contributed to greater income inequality aand poverty persisted in Ghana.

<u>Thesis 3: Market-based policies do not address barriers to development like weak institutional frameworks</u>

1. The Democratic Republic of the Congo (DRC) is one of the world's richest countries in terms of natural resources, and is responsible for possessing around 70% of the world's cobalt production. Despite this, the DRC ranks one of the lowest in the world in GDP (PPP) per capita and HDI.

2. 97.5% of all workers in the DRC work in the informal economy, including about 200,000 miners. Chinese MNCs which export a majority of copper and cobalt from the DRC do so with miners who work in unsafe conditions, without any safety materials and exposed to toxic substances.

3. The lack of government regulations and standards is exacerbated by prevalent use of child labour.

4. Corrupt civil servants also frequent markets in the DRC to extort fabricated taxes, and both legitimate and fake taxes are pocketed rather than being given to the government, limiting the government funds available for social programs and infrastructure.

5. Small businesses in the DRC are also afraid to expand as they become more prone to being targeted for extortion by corrupt government officials. This not only prevents businesses from achieving economies of scale, but also makes them unwilling to register and enter the formal economy.

6. Yet, without registering their businesses, they have lower credit ratings and thus find it harder to access credit and insurance. These self-employed individuals cannot obtain the funds to finance business investments as well as healthcare and education, thus remaining trapped in the poverty cycle (Fig 2).

7. Market-based policies do not address but exacerbate these issues. Working conditions (especially in mining) will continue to be poor. Making markets more competitive does not stop corruption and embezzlement of tax revenue.

Antithesis 1: Competition promotes efficiency

1. Market-based policies such as privatisation and deregulation make markets more competitive as they improve the price mechanism's signalling and incentive functions, maximising social surplus and improving allocative efficiency. Firms are also incentivised to lower costs, improving productive efficiency.

2. In the 1990s, India allowed the private sector to enter the telecoms sector and compete with the state-owned BSNL, which had a monopoly on Indian telecommunications. Regulations on obtaining licences were eased allowing more private operators to enter the sector and compete.

3. By introducing competition, telecom providers were incentivised to cut costs while also investing in more efficient and up-to-date technologies. This helped to spur the adoption of mobile telecoms and shift away from traditional landlines across India, as well as adoption of internet services by the 2000s.

4. With competition, prices for telecom services were lowered and became more affordable. Eventually, most middle-class families in India were able to afford cell phones.

5. Lower prices for telecommunications, including mobile services and internet, meant that much more rural villages in India had access, improving connectivity with urban areas and reducing the rural-urban digital divide.

6. India now has close to 1.2 billion wireless telephone subscribers and 750 million broadband internet subscribers, of which rural subscribers make up around 45%.

7. Faster and easier telecommunications allows economic activity to be carried out more efficiently, and lower prices also promotes inclusive participation in economic activity as rural areas are better connected.

8. In addition, as more telecom firms enter the market to compete, investment spending (I) is stimulated, causing aggregate demand (AD) to increase from AD_0 to AD_1, as in Fig 3. Furthermore, improved efficiency across the board leads to potential output increasing from Y_{f0} to Y_{f1} and the Keynesian Aggregate Supply (AS) curve shifting rightwards from AS_0 to AS_1.

9. The overall increase in real GDP from Y_0 to Y_1 shows the sustained economic growth from India's privatisation and deregulation of the telecoms sector.

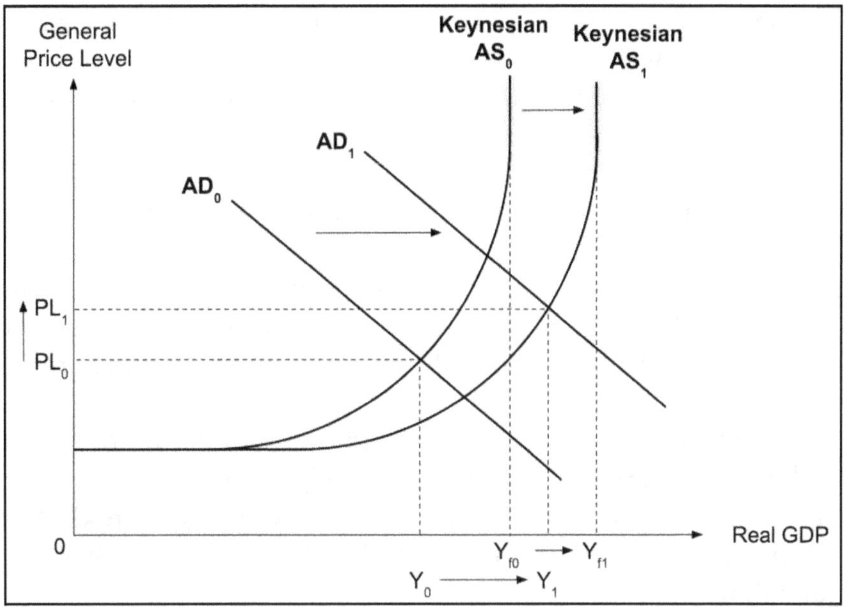

Fig 3: sustained growth from privatising and deregulating telecoms

10. With economic growth, the derived demand for labour by firms also increases, leading to higher employment and wages. As in Fig 2, this leads to greater incomes, improving material well-being.

11. Rural and poorer areas also benefit greatly as telemedicine improves access to healthcare, while students in rural areas can also receive higher-quality education through online platforms. These both increase the human capital of those living in rural areas, which as in Fig 2 improves their productivity and helps them escape the poverty trap too while also improving non-material well-being.

<u>Antithesis 2: Floating exchange rates</u>

1. Floating exchange rate system is one that allows the value of the currency to be determined by market forces of supply and demand.

2. When Peru abandoned its exchange rate peg in 1990 and moved to a managed float, its reserves had almost been depleted. Without a currency peg, developing countries like Peru would not need to have large foreign reserves to defend the currency peg.

3. The depletion of foreign reserves reduces Peru's ability to import consumer goods and services, thus reducing standard of living. It also reduces her ability to import capital goods, which would have helped grow her economy and spur economic development.

4. Additionally, without the peg, the central bank had greater flexibility over use of monetary policy as interest rates no longer had to be in line to maintain the currency peg. Peru could then increase interest rates to tame hyperinflation at the time.

5. Inflation was brought down from over 7000% in 1990 to 3.5% by 1999.

6. If Peru had stuck with its currency peg, increasing interest rates would attract hot money inflows from foreign investors, which increases the demand for the Peruvian sol, placing an upward pressure on the exchange rate.

7. To lower the exchange rate back to its pegged value, the central bank would then have to intervene by buying foreign reserves and selling more sol to increase the supply of sol in the foreign exchange (forex) market; this would end up increasing the money supply, reducing interest rates and failing to tackle inflation.

Concluding Section

1. While market-based policies can promote growth and development, its shortcomings mean that developing countries should not only implement market-based policies. Some degree of government intervention is also needed, as evidenced by the presence of market failures like negative environmental externalities and under-allocation of resources to merit goods, as aforementioned.

2. Yet, as excessive government intervention in markets may lead to inefficiencies and other distortions, a good balance of market-based policies and intervention is needed to promote development in ELDCs.

8. Using real world examples, discuss the extent to which foreign aid is the key to economic development for ELDCs. (15)

Introduction

1. Economic development is the sustained improvement in both material and non-material economic well-being of residents in a country.

2. Material well-being refers to the quantity and quality of goods & services available for consumption to consumers.

3. Non-material well-being refers to less tangible quality of life factors, such as education and health standards, gender equality, and environmental quality.

4. Foreign aid is the transfer of funds in the form of loans or grants, or transfer of goods & services as gifts to economically least developed countries (ELDCs) to help them achieve economic or social objectives.

5. Foreign aid is concessional, meaning that these transfers involve more favourable conditions than could be achieved in the market. For example, aid given as loans are given at lower-than-market interest rates and have longer repayment periods.

6. Foreign aid can be in the form of Official Development Assistance (ODA), which is offered by countries or by international organisations such as the International Monetary Fund (IMF) and the World Bank.

7. Aid could also be provided by Non-Governmental Organisations (NGOs), which are non-profit and provide grants to ELDCs.

Thesis 1: Aid can plug the savings-investment gap boosting economic growth and reducing poverty

1. Grants or loans, such as aid for infrastructure projects, can help ELDCs break the savings-investment gap.

2. In ELDCs, since incomes are typically low, people have low levels of savings which leads to very little funds banks can lend out to firms for investment, limiting economic growth and incomes as shown in the poverty cycle below

(Fig 1).

3. ODA could provide the funds that firms in ELDCs need for investment in basic infrastructure.

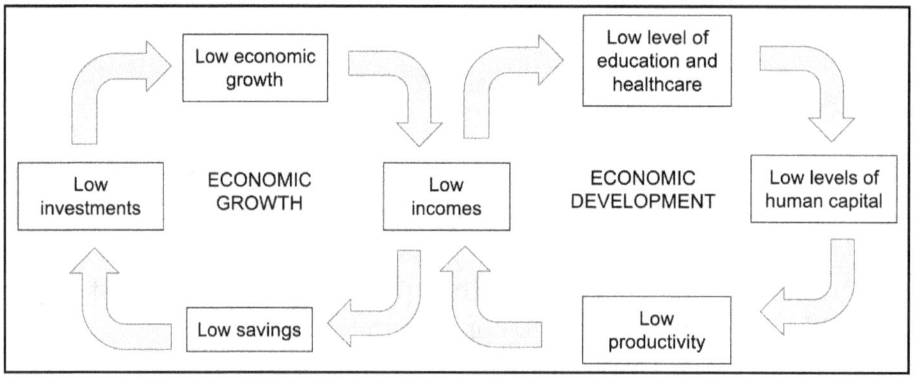

Fig 1: poverty cycle diagram

4. For example, in 2020, the World Bank gave US$150 million in ODA to Rwanda to improve access to electricity for households and firms, while also promoting sustainable energy and reducing reliance on pollutive cooking oil.

5. The aid increase investment (I) as energy firms expand capacity and government spending on infrastructure, thus increasing Aggregate Demand from AD_0 to AD_1. Greater access to electricity also tend to increase productivity leading to potential output increasing from Y_{f0} to Y_{f1}. Real GDP, determined from where the Aggregate Demand (AD) curve intersects the Keynesian Aggregate Supply (AS) curve, thus increases from Y_0 to Y_1.

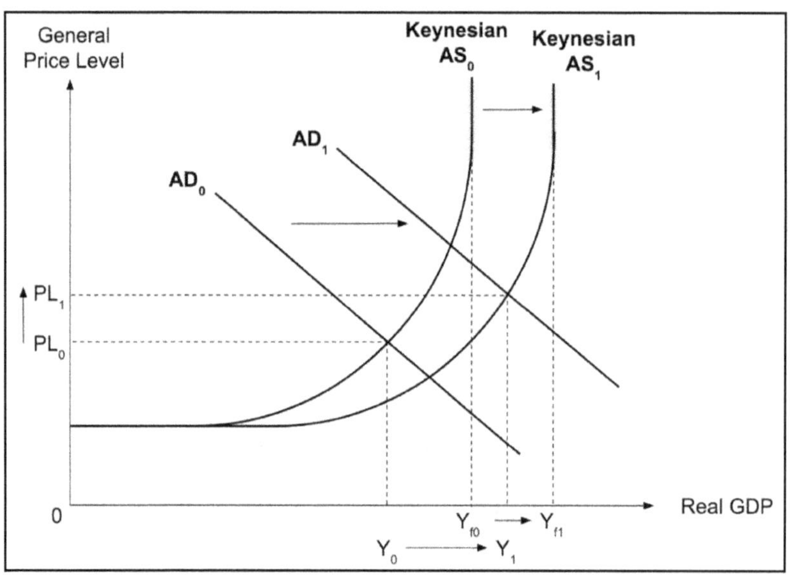

Fig 2: sustained economic growth from ODA

6. The sustained growth in real output is met with an increase in the derived demand for labour, thus increasing employment. With income, more consumption of healthcare and education services can take place, increasing productivity and further increasing incomes allowing the people in Rwanda to break out of the poverty cycle shown in Fig 1.

7. Furthermore, promoting sustainable energy for households also helps improve environmental quality in the longer term. These can both contribute to higher non-material well-being and sustainable development.

Thesis 2: Aid can be targeted

1. Aid funds, either by ODA or by NGOs, can be targeted towards the most needy in society to help improve their access to healthcare and education, improving their non-material well-being as well as increasing human capital, productivity and thus the ability to earn higher incomes.

2. This helps the poor break out of the poverty cycle.

3. For example, UNICEF (an NGO) provides funds directed to impoverished children (and pregnant mothers) in ELDCs for immunisations, prevention of diseases like HIV and AIDS, as well as improving nutrition.

4. Another example is the World Bank providing ODA worth US$1.5 billion for investments in education programs in Punjab, Pakistan since 2003.

5. With the ODA, the number of children enrolled in school increased dramatically from 15 million (2003) to 26 million in 2020. The gender disparity in enrollment was also reduced and many more girls have also been able to enrol in school, with the 78% girls' enrollment rate in Punjab far higher than the rest of Pakistan (56%) in 2020.

6. Not only are more children able to escape the poverty cycle (Fig 1) in the long term, improving education for girls also helps them become better mothers. As females tend to be the caretakers of children, better educated mothers can help to reduce child mortality, increasing non-material welfare.

7. With better education, more females will also have access to better employment opportunities, reducing income inequality between genders which also promotes development.

Thesis 3: Foreign aid can help ELDCs relieve their debt

1. The concessional nature of foreign aid also helps highly indebted ELDCs relieve their debt. For example, the Heavily Indebted Poor Countries (HIPC) initiative by the World Bank and IMF helps certain ELDCs cancel a portion of their external debt.

2. This helps them escape the debt trap of borrowing more to service old debts.

3. Relieving their debt burden allows ELDCs to reallocate funds and resources to promote development, such as developing rural infrastructure, and providing basic healthcare and education.

4. For example, at the start of the COVID-19 Pandemic in 2020, the IMF approved a grant of US$14.3 million to relieve Tanzania of its debt burden. This then helped free up tax revenues which the government could then spend on the healthcare system, such as investments in more medical equipment and supplies, improving medical facilities, and hiring more medical staff.

5. This helped improve Tanzanians' urgently needed access to healthcare to deal with the pandemic, allowing citizens to remain healthier.

6. Furthermore, the pandemic caused Tanzania's tourism and service sectors to contract, resulting in recession and higher unemployment.

7. The debt relief allowed the Tanzanian government to ramp up spending on social protection as well as support for small businesses and those in poverty (including the newly unemployed), preventing a poverty crisis.

Antithesis 1: Tied & conditional aid

1. Donor countries may provide aid with certain conditions that the ELDCs must meet.

2. Aid is often tied, meaning that the recipients of aid must spend either all or a portion of the borrowed funds to buy goods & services from the donor country.

3. Tied aid results in higher import costs for the ELDCs since they cannot then seek lower price alternatives for the goods & services needed. The OECD estimates that tied aid can increase the cost of development projects by 15 to 30%.

4. This creates opportunity costs for ELDCs in the form of forgoing spending on more meaningful development projects such as providing healthcare.

5. For example, China has given out many developmental loans to East African ELDCs for projects like transport and power infrastructure, and 87.3% of these loans are concessional and could qualify as aid. However, the construction contracts are mostly awarded to Chinese firms which then import Chinese capital goods, and in some cases bring in Chinese labour as well. Less competition in the awarding of the contracts could thus add to the costs for the recipient country and there may be fewer employment opportunities for the Africans than expected.

6. Additionally, conditional aid may force ELDCs to implement structural changes which may not be appropriate for the ELDC in question.

7. The IMF and World Bank have historically provided aid on the condition that market-based policies and austerity policies must be implemented.

8. For example, in the 1980s and 1990s, Ghana received loans from the World Bank while carrying out privatisation and trade liberalisation pushed for by the World Bank.

9. It led to greater unemployment due to increased competition and firms cutting labour costs. As a result, income inequality actually increased and poverty persisted.

10. Cutting government spending also led to reduced provision of merit goods like healthcare in Ghana which poor people in rural areas already struggled to have access to. Healthcare costs increased by 800 to 1000%, leaving many households unable to access this basic necessity.

11. In Ghana's case, while it did experience real GDP growth, the effects on the non-material well-being of Ghanaians and income inequality ended up being questionable.

<u>Antithesis 2: Over-reliance on aid</u>

1. ELDCs may also become overreliant on aid and some governments may end up not doing enough effort on their own, resulting in detrimental effects in the long-term.

2. An example of this is Malawi, where 81% of the country's total expenditure in the healthcare sector comes from foreign aid.

3. This leaves Malawi highly vulnerable to donors' changing budget priorities, which makes the flow of aid to Malawi unpredictable. As a result, access to healthcare remains limited and unpredictable.

4. Aid in the form of goods & services from donors could end up also substituting domestic goods & services, inhibiting local production and growth. This has been the case with previous food aid in Haiti.

5. Reliance on food imports from the US reduced the demand for domestically produced foods, causing many farmers to go out of business and seek employment in assembly plants instead. Even as food aid stopped, Haiti continued to be reliant on food imports and when global food prices increased, became unaffordable to many.

Antithesis 3: Foreign aid's effectiveness is limited by corruption

1. In ELDCs with high levels of corruption, aid funds may be embezzled or not used effectively to promote development.

2. From 2002 to 2019, Afghanistan received US$76.6 billion worth of ODA from the US. However, much of the ODA was embezzled and pocketed by elites in Afghanistan and was not used to help the poor.

3. Corrupt officials also diverted ODA funds towards funding Afghanistan's opium industry. Over 40% of agricultural land is now dedicated to opium production, producing over 85% of the world's opium.

4. Institutional corruption in the education system also reduces the effectiveness of ODA in improving education, with widespread bribery leading to incompetent and underqualified teachers providing low-quality education. "Ghost" schools were also set up across the country to embezzle foreign aid funds.

5. Despite all the aid, Afghanistan's Human Development Index (HDI) still ranked very low globally at 169th of 189 in 2019.

Concluding Section

1. While foreign aid does have its criticisms, such as conditionality and over-reliance, aid may still be important for promoting development in ELDCs, for lack of better alternatives. Without aid, ELDCs will continue to struggle with low savings and high debt, which definitely limit development.

2. Yet, aid alone cannot be the key. Other strategies to promote economic growth and development should be implemented, together with inflows of foreign aid.

3. Botswana is an example of this, successfully achieving development and becoming a middle income country. Despite being heavily dependent on foreign aid initially, strategies like Aid for Trade, low corruption and good governance ultimately helped it develop.

9. Explain the relationship between poverty and sustainability. (10)

Introduction

1. Poverty is the inability of consumers or families to satisfy basic physical needs, such as food, clothing, and shelter, due to low incomes.

2. Sustainability refers to the ability of the present generation to satisfy its needs, without reducing future generations' ability to satisfy their needs.

3. Worldwide, a lack of environmental sustainability exacerbates the difficulties that impoverished families face in escaping the poverty trap, which may in turn also contribute to greater environmental damage.

Poor families tend to depend on the environment for income and are more greatly affected by resource depletion

1. According to the UN Environment Programme, 70% of the world's poor draw upon natural resources for most of their livelihoods. Farmlands, grasslands, forests, freshwaters, and oceans are the sources for more than half of the income of poor households worldwide.

2. Yet most of these resources are common pool resources – resources that are non-excludable but rivalrous, meaning that it is not possible to exclude someone from using the good (such as by setting a price), and usage reduces the resource's availability for others.

3. For example, deforestation occurs since forests and trees lack a chargeable price for being cut down, and are thus being depleted, cleared for land use and for selling timber.

4. As the forest's resources are too rapidly harvested and not given enough time to replenish itself, this reduces the amount of resources available to the poor, directly reducing their income sources, thereby entrenching them further in poverty, including their future generations who will have to compete more greatly for these increasingly scarce resources.

5. As seen in Fig 1 below, unable to earn more income, they will continue to lack the ability to accumulate human and physical capital and even enhance

natural capital, continuing in a lack of productivity and so perpetuating the poverty trap.

6. Being stuck in the poverty trap only worsens the depletion of natural resources as the poor are forced to further exploit the already scarce natural resources which depletes them further.

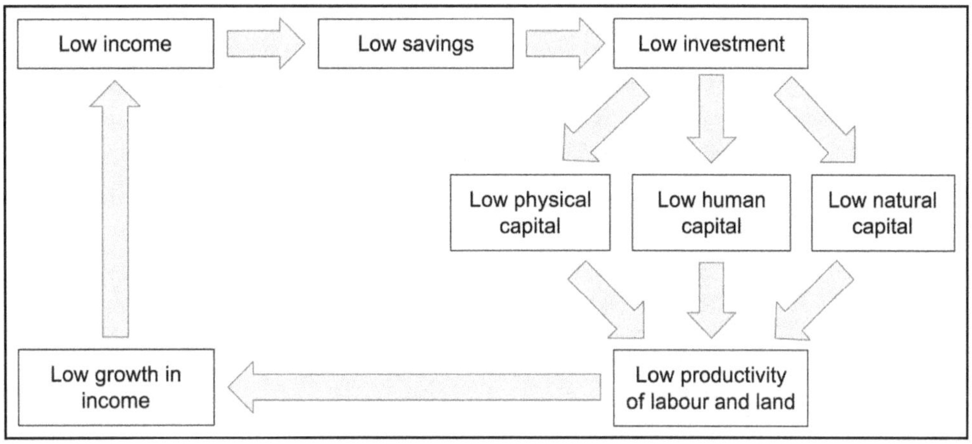

Fig 1: the poverty trap

<u>Poor communities lack the resources to mitigate the effects of environmental unsustainability</u>

1. Poor people often also do not own their land and lack land tenure. Coupled with insufficient knowledge of good agricultural practices and the inability to afford irrigation and fertilisers will likely lead to low levels of agricultural productivity and crop yields. This is another vicious cycle as their poverty will push them to over-exploiting more lands with consequences of greater areas of soil erosion and land degradation.

2. The threat is not only to the low-income households, but to the long-term sustainability of the land as a natural resource.

3. Poor countries are also the ones that are least likely to be able to afford the costs of mitigation needed to avert the climate crisis. Poor communities also lack the resources to adapt to extreme weather events and environmental catastrophes caused by climate change.

4. These communities may live in areas prone to flooding, landslides, and rising sea levels, yet lack the financial resources to move to less vulnerable areas. They then have to spend a larger portion of their income to recover from these events, such as to rebuild destroyed homes, further perpetuating their poverty.

5. Thus, the climate crisis will continue to have a disproportionate effect on the poor.

10. Using real world examples, evaluate the advantages and disadvantages of membership in a common market. (15)

Introduction

1. Within a common market, members agree to eliminate all restrictions on movement of factors of production like labour and capital.

2. This is on top of members removing tariffs and other trade barriers between them, as well as adopting a common external trade policy towards all non-members.

3. Examples of common markets include the European Single Market and Mercosur (consisting of several South American countries).

Advantage 1: Improved resource allocation and economic growth

1. In member countries with high demand for labour, they will easily be able to attract workers from other member countries where unemployment is high. This is because workers are free to move and work in any member country without restrictions.

2. Workers will also have greater employment opportunities as a result, reducing unemployment or underemployment and being able to make full use of their skills, becoming more productive.

3. In the European Single Market, high labour mobility allows labour shortages in certain industries to be filled by workers from other members.

4. Labour shortages in mining and construction in Italy, France, and the Netherlands are filled by workers from countries like Romania and Poland. Meanwhile, shortages of higher-skilled science and engineering professionals in Germany and Spain are partially filled by workers from other members too.

5. The lack of restrictions on movement of financial capital and cross-border investments allows financial capital to flow towards countries where investments are more profitable, making better use of financial resources.

6. In the European Single Market, the general lack of capital controls allows large amounts of financial capital to freely flow between members.

7. As a result, companies can easily sell stocks and bonds to investors across Europe, while banks across Europe can loan out funds for projects and businesses in other member states.

8. Firms can thus more easily expand into the wider common market, being able to take advantage of not only more productive labour, but also possibly cheaper factors of production like physical capital and labour.

9. Countries like Slovakia benefit from firms expanding into their country. Upon joining the European Single Market in 2004, foreign direct investment (FDI) inflows rose dramatically as manufacturing multinational corporations (MNCs) began expanding into Slovakia to take advantage of lower-wage labour.

10. With greater FDI inflows, investment expenditure (I) increased causing Aggregate Demand (AD) to increase from AD_0 to AD_1 as in Fig 1 below.

11. Furthermore, labour within Slovakia became more productively employed. Higher-skilled labour could leave Slovakia and search for better job opportunities elsewhere in Europe, while lower-skilled labour began to be employed by the foreign manufacturing MNCs. From 2004 to 2008, unemployment nearly halved from 18.2% to 9.5%.

12. These MNCs also increased competition for domestic producers, spurring increases in efficiency as domestic producers are incentivised to lower costs to remain profitable.

13. Both the increases in labour productivity and productive efficiency lead to the potential output of the economy increasing from Y_{f0} to Y_{f1}, as shown in Fig 1 below.

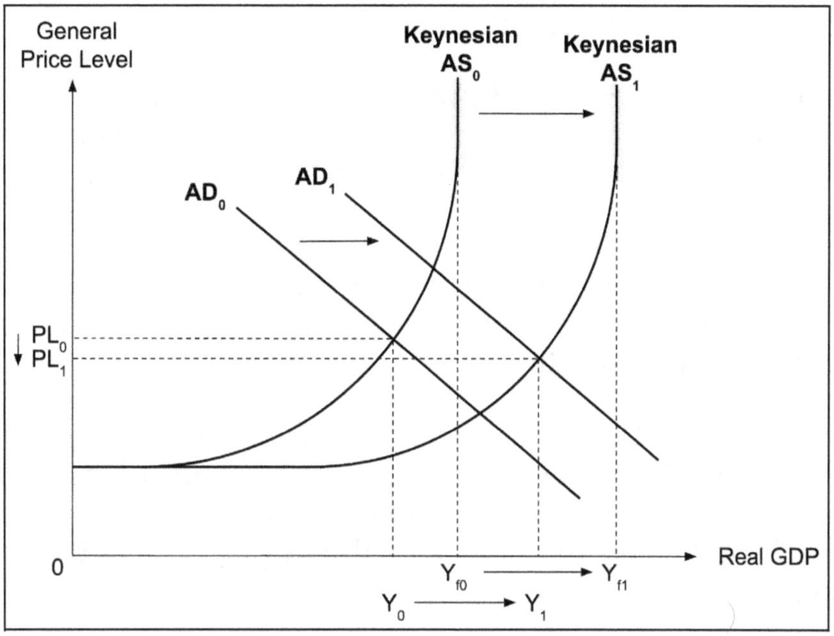

Fig 1: sustained growth from joining common market

14. The increase in real GDP from Y_0 to Y_1 represents actual economic growth experienced by Slovakia, which increased from 5.3% in 2004 to 10.8% in 2007.

Advantage 2: Greater efficiency and competition lowers consumer prices

1. In addition to the increased competition spurring efficiency, the enlarged market also allows firms to expand and achieve economies of scale and reduce their average costs to an even greater extent. For example, through bulk buying of raw materials, bulk discounts could be achieved, lowering unit costs.

2. With production costs lowered and increased competition, consumer prices should decrease as a result and goods become more affordable. Together with a wider variety of goods from which consumers can choose, this thus means that consumers should experience greater material welfare.

3. For example, automakers in Mercosur, particularly those from Brazil, benefit from economies of scale as they can expand into the enlarged Mercosur market, thus being able to produce at competitive prices. This then lowers consumer prices for automobiles across countries in Mercosur as other producers must also lower prices to be able to compete with the Brazilian automakers.

Advantage 3: Spread of technology across the common market

1. In the European Single Market, free mobility of labour allows skilled tech professionals to be able to move freely across member states and find employment, especially in countries where there is higher demand for such skilled labour.

2. Firms located in a member country can then employ the expertise provided by tech professionals from across the entire single market, becoming more productive and innovative.

3. For example, Ireland attracts many tech firms, both MNCs and startups, to set up bases in their country, attracting many skilled tech professionals from across Europe. The "import" of technological know-how has helped develop Ireland's technology sector greatly, also helping Ireland become a tech hub in Europe.

4. With no restrictions on FDI within the single market, more rapid technology transfers and widespread adoption of new technologies can be achieved within the bloc, boosting economic growth for member countries. When one grows, through exports, other countries' growth can also be spurred, thus benefitting all member countries.

Disadvantage 1: Some members may experience an outflow of resources, especially labour

1. While, as mentioned, labour can be reallocated to meet shortages in different member countries, wage differences between different members in a common market can result in labour flowing out of lower-wage countries into higher-wage countries.

2. With freedom of movement for labour guaranteed within the European single market, this makes it easier for Polish workers to relocate to other member countries like the UK and Germany, where there are better job opportunities and higher wages thus allowing these workers to earn higher incomes.

3. This not only includes low-skilled labour like construction workers and cleaners, but also affects certain higher-skilled sectors like medical doctors too.

4. The outflow of labour then creates labour shortages in the affected sectors in Poland. Firms then face higher labour costs as a result of competing for increasingly scarce labour. This is evident from the difficulty by firms to fill job vacancies in Poland despite low unemployment rates. As a result, the

economy's productive capacity may shrink and economic growth may be retarded.

5. In the macroeconomy, this would be recessionary and drive up inflation as seen below with the AS curve falling from AS_0 to AS_1, causing the real GDP to fall from Y_0 to Y_1 and the general price level to increase from PL_0 to PL_1.

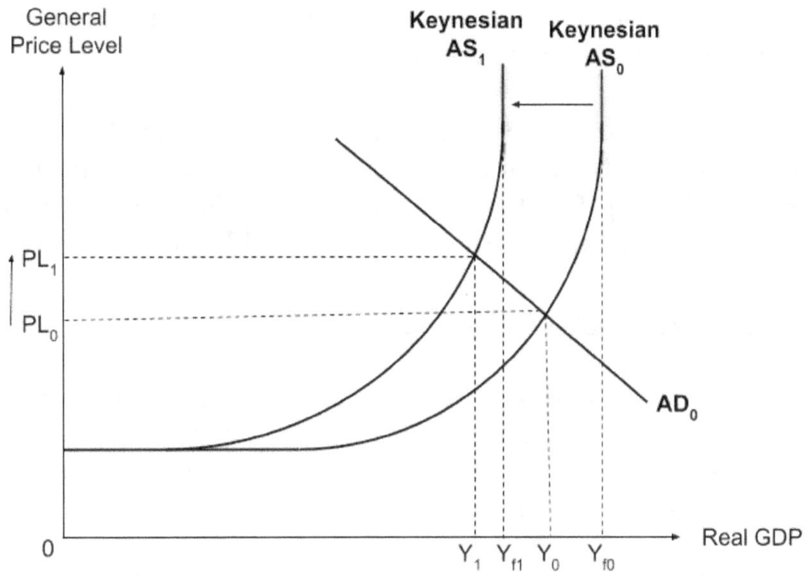

Fig 2: recessionary effect of outflow of labour

6. For lower-wage countries in the common market, the shortages created from the outflow of labour would not be corrected until wages have been adjusted upwards, however this may take a long time to achieve.

7. Poland, which joined the European single market in 2004, only started seeing the net outflow of labour stop in 2019 as a result of improved wages and lower costs of living, compared to other single market members.

<u>Disadvantage 2: Workers may not benefit from greater competition</u>

1. In the same example mentioned earlier (*Advantage 2*), as Brazilian automakers become more efficient from economies of scale in Mercosur, automakers in Argentina then face greater competition from these lower-cost Brazilian imports, especially since Argentina is the largest export market for Brazilian automakers.

2. Argentinian automakers then face pressures to lower costs so as to maintain profitability. Domestic Argentinian automakers may do so by lowering wages or may even have to retrench workers entirely. This can lead to higher rates of structural unemployment as the workers may lack the skills to take on jobs in growing sectors.

3. In another example, Siemens (2004) took advantage of the European Single Market's freedom of mobility for goods and capital to shift its production lines and physical capital from two factories in Germany to Hungary to take advantage of lower labour costs. 2,000 jobs in Germany were cut as a result, with further wage cuts for other workers.

4. The lower incomes by workers in both cases leads to lower disposable incomes and ability to purchase goods & services, thus resulting in lower material well-being for these workers. They also become more vulnerable to falling into poverty, especially if they are unable to transition into new jobs.

<u>Disadvantage 3: Trade diversion (HL Only)</u>

1. A common external trade policy, together with removal of all trade barriers between members in a common market may encourage trade diversion away from low-cost imports from non-member countries towards higher-cost producers within the common market.

2. For example, Mercosur's common external tariff (CET) has led to the automotive industry in the bloc being highly protected, leading to trade diversion.

3. Due to tariffs, automobiles produced outside Mercosur become more expensive compared to automobiles produced in member countries, especially those from Brazilian producers which achieved economies of scale as mentioned.

4. Globally, more scarce resources are then allocated to producers within Mercosur which are relatively less efficient compared to other global producers, worsening resource allocation.

5. Social surplus for member countries like Argentina is also reduced as the price for importing from Brazilian producers is higher than the price of importing from other producers without the CET.

Concluding Section

1. Different members in the common market will experience different, and possibly unequal benefits as well. For example, while Poland was hurt by labour outflows upon joining the European SingleMmarket, higher-income members like the UK benefited from having these relatively lower-wage Polish workers.

2. However, the increased mobility of labour & capital and the enlarged markets for firms to expand into can lead to long-term benefits for member economies (like sustained growth), which could exceed the more short-term costs.

3. Even for Poland, the FDI inflows and the accompanying transfer of tech and expertise resulted in sustained real GDP growth.

4. Member economies in a common market could also experience even more benefits if the bloc seeks other forms of economic integration with other countries or blocs. Negotiating as a common market provides greater bargaining power to achieve more preferable trade and other concessions.

5. Mercosur and the EU, for example, agreed in 2019 on a proposed free trade agreement which would lead to larger export markets for Mercosur agricultural products and cheaper imports of capital goods from Europe. At the same time, EU producers could obtain cheaper raw materials from Mercosur and have increased exports of secondary goods like chemicals, pharmaceuticals, and cars. For both blocs, real output could then increase leading to economic growth on both sides.

11. Using real world examples, discuss the effects of rising public sector debt in low income countries. (15)

Introduction

1. Public sector debt is money borrowed by a country's government to finance welfare programs and government policies.

2. Such funds can be borrowed from internal lenders such as banks through issuing bonds and treasury bills, or from external lenders such as the World Bank, the International Monetary Fund (IMF), or other countries.

3. Low income countries, such as economically least developed countries (ELDCs), tend to have high levels of debt as they lack the necessary tax revenue to finance infrastructure and other government projects.

Thesis 1: External borrowing can fill the savings-investment gap to fund development projects

1. In Ethiopia, an ELDC, the low level of savings from low incomes resulted in the country being dependent on external borrowing to finance its development.

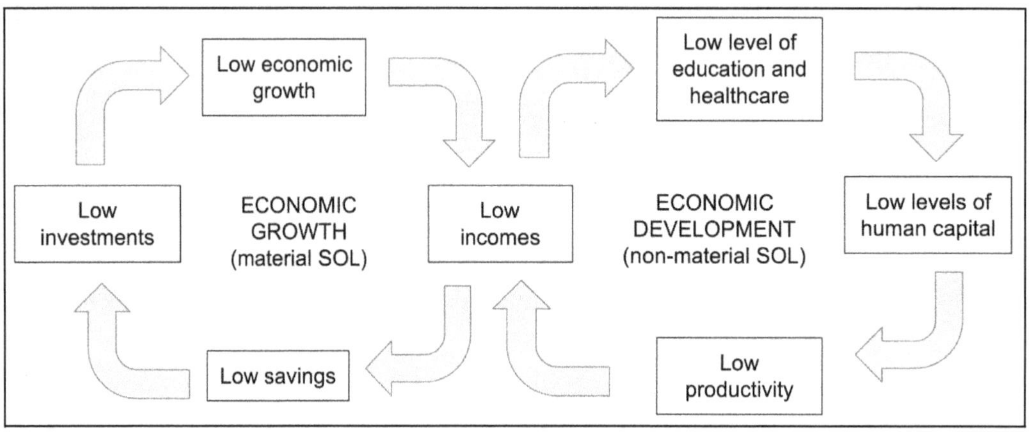

Fig 1: the poverty cycle

2. The low level of savings means that banks do not have the necessary funds to loan out to firms to finance investment projects. As in the poverty cycle shown above (Fig 1), this further stunts economic growth in the country as real output growth is limited, causing people to continue being stuck with low

incomes.

3. External borrowing instead directly provides the funds needed for the Ethiopian government to invest in increasing its road density, electricity generation capacity, and number of schools and hospitals.

4. Increasing road infrastructure improves mobility of resources such as physical capital and labour, therefore improving productivity as less time and effort is wasted in transporting them, allowing these resources to be better employed.

5. Increasing electricity generation capacity was also met with an increase in access to electricity, from 12.7% (2000) to 51.1% (2020) of the population. As a basic need for carrying out daily activities, this not only improves workers' standard of living, but also improves productivity as electricity enables economic activity and production.

6. Increasing the number of schools and hospitals allows people greater access to education and healthcare, improving their human capital (Fig 1) as they become better educated and healthier. This increases their non-material standard of living and improves productivity.

7. With the external borrowing improving productivity, workers are able to earn higher incomes and break out of the poverty cycle (Fig 1), also experiencing increases to their material standard of living as their purchasing power increases.

8. With increases in both material and non-material standard of living, Ethiopia's external borrowing thus finances projects which do lead to economic development. From 2000 to 2020, when Ethiopia's investments in development projects were financed by external debt, the country's Human Development Index (HDI) also increased from 0.287 to 0.498.

<u>Thesis 2: Debt funds can also be used to spur growth through diversification</u>

1. While Rwanda has historically been dependent on exports of primary goods such as coffee, tea, and minerals, from the 2000s it has started to diversify away from such primary goods towards more value-added goods & services. In 2000, gold, coffee, tea, zirconium ore and tin ore (all primary goods) made up 96% of Rwanda's exports, but this number has fallen to 61% in 2020. The country has done this through using some of its public sector debt.

2. Primary goods tend to be more price-volatile as they have low Price Elasticity of Demand (PED) and Price Elasticity of Supply (PES) values, which leads to

unstable export revenue and thus unstable growth.

3. Government spending on aggressive marketing campaigns has allowed Rwanda's coffee and tea sectors to shift towards niche, specialty markets. This has afforded these sectors more protection from volatile global prices, and export revenues for Rwanda's coffee and tea actually increased despite world prices for these goods falling.

4. The Rwandan economy has also diversified away to other sectors like manufacturing and services (which grew to account for 43% of the country's GDP in 2010), and this is thanks to government investments in these sectors.

5. For example, the government funded the setting up of the Kigali Special Economic Zone (KSEZ) to better attract manufacturing firms to build production facilities for value-added goods (mainly for import substitution but also for exports) within the KSEZ.

6. Construction of the Kigali International Financial Centre also marked the start of diversification into the banking and finance sector. Rwanda has also invested even more into tourism, which accounts for more than 70% of service exports. This includes construction of the Kigali Convention Center and large investments in global marketing campaigns.

7. High value-added goods and services have sustained increases in demand globally. Thus, utilising public sector debt to invest and diversify towards such sectors can help low income countries like Rwanda achieve stable economic growth. From 2000 to 2019, Rwanda managed to consistently experience around 8% annual growth in GDP.

Thesis 3: Debt funds can be used to deal with emergencies

1. Due to either low incomes, poor taxation structures, or both, ELDCs tend to have insufficient tax revenue for government spending. This becomes problematic when emergencies such as natural disasters occur as the government then does not have the resources to deal with such emergencies.

2. These countries then turn to borrowing, typically both bilaterally and multilaterally, so as to finance recovery efforts.

3. When Pakistan was hit with the massive 2005 Kashmir earthquake, apart from having a very high number of casualties, 500,000 families were also affected and 4 million were left homeless. Infrastructure such as roads, schools, hospitals and other buildings were also destroyed, with reconstruction costs

alone estimated at US$3 billion.

4. Without enough government funds to finance providing food and shelter for the displaced and rebuilding infrastructure, Pakistan's government turned to external borrowing from the World Bank and the Asian Development Bank, as well as from other bilateral partners like China and the US.

5. These funds could then be directly used to provide basic necessities such as food, water, and shelter for the displaced, ensuring that they have enough for survival and preventing them from falling into extreme poverty.

6. Apart from this, the borrowed funds were also used to rebuild infrastructure like roads, which are necessary for productive economic activity. Schools and hospitals were also rebuilt using the borrowed funds; both are merit goods necessary for improvements in human capital through providing education and healthcare, helping people escape the poverty cycle as in Fig 1.

7. Therefore, when emergencies happen, public sector debt may be crucial in allowing economic activity to continue as well as preventing standards of living from falling, thus allowing growth and development to continue.

<u>Antithesis 1: ELDCs may struggle to repay the public sector debt</u>

1. When low income countries like ELDCs borrow large amounts to finance projects, the debt may end up increasing to an unsustainable level, causing the country in question to struggle to repay it.

2. In 2022, Ghana's debt-to-GDP ratio grew to 92.4%. Debt servicing was taking up more than half of the government's total revenue and 70% of tax revenues.

3. Ghana's high public sector debt meant that the government had little resources to provide merit goods like education, healthcare, and infrastructure, since most of its revenue was directly being used to repay its debts.

4. With provision of education and healthcare being directly hindered, as in the poverty cycle (Fig 1), workers are unable to improve their human capital and be more productive, thus reducing their ability to earn income and break out of poverty, hindering development. Furthermore, as mentioned earlier (*Thesis 1*), infrastructure such as roads improves productivity, thus if the government is unable to provide or maintain such infrastructure then development is similarly hindered.

5. ELDCs like Ghana are then forced to increase government revenue such as through increasing income taxes, but the revenue generated is limited since incomes are already low.

6. Increasing income taxes for lower-income earners is not only politically unpopular but also goes against development. Their disposable incomes would fall, leading to lower material welfare since it then becomes more difficult to afford necessities. This is also adverse for economic growth, since consumption (C), a component of Aggregate Demand (AD) and thus real GDP, would fall, leading to higher unemployment and even more poverty.

7. Investments in human capital, such as education & healthcare, also become more expensive which then reduces non-material welfare as well as hindering development, as seen in the poverty cycle (Fig 1).

8. With the higher public sector debt, Ghana's S&P credit ratings were also downgraded, causing the government's creditworthiness to fall. Investors then have lower confidence in the government's ability to repay its debts (like bonds and securities), leading to lower inward investment and greater capital flight, reducing the amount of funds available in the economy, weakening economic growth and thus development.

9. With large public sector debt, ELDCs like Ghana may fall into a debt trap, where they keep on taking out larger loans to service old debts. Ghana had to seek a US$3 billion loan from the IMF (the lender of last resort) to resolve its debt woes.

<u>Antithesis 2: Internal borrowing leads to crowding out of private investment</u>

1. In Malawi, an ELDC, most of its government spending has been financed by internal borrowing. While such spending has been on subsidies on agricultural inputs for domestic farmers, education, and infrastructure, the internal borrowing has also led to crowding out of private investment.

2. Malawi has the 3rd lowest GNI per capita in the world and over 70% live in absolute poverty. The low income levels result in very low tax revenue generated, thus increasing the government's reliance on borrowing from banks to finance its spending.

3. However, government borrowing increases the demand for money, which then leads to higher interest rates. This then stunts investment by firms in the private sector as they face higher costs of borrowing to finance projects, lower rate of returns and lower profitability. Domestic small and medium enterprises

(SMEs) thus struggle to operate as a result of this limited credit availability.

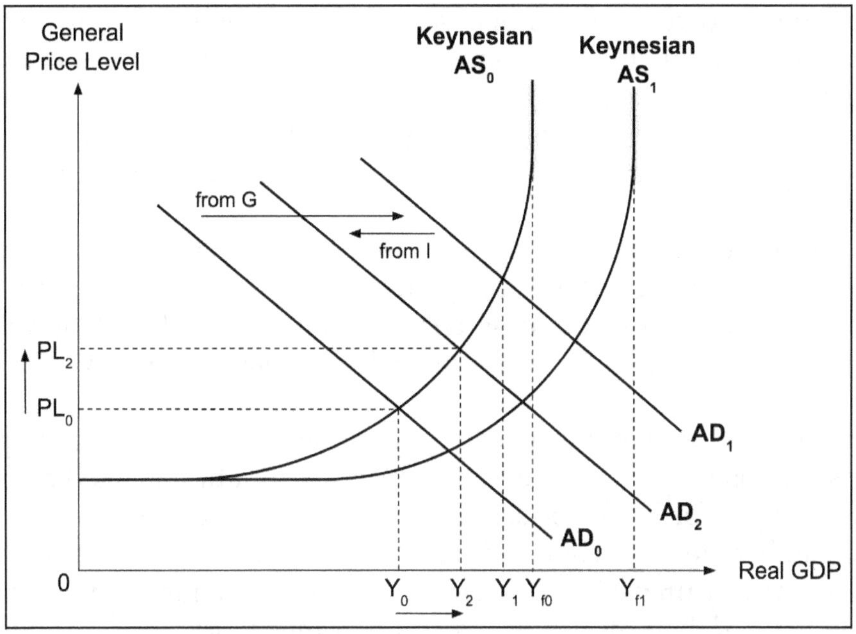

Fig 2: crowding out preventing sustained growth

4. While the government spending (G) alone could increase the aggregate demand from AD_0 to AD_1, the reduced investment (I) by firms could partially offset that, causing aggregate demand to only increase from AD_1 to AD_2. It could have even resulted in AD not increasing at all.

5. Likewise, while the government spending (G) on infrastructure and education also increases productivity and could therefore increase the potential output from Y_{f0} to Y_{f1}, this could be negated by the reduced private sector investment as firms are less able to invest in capital goods.

Antithesis 3: Higher debt leads to more exchange rate risks

1. If the public sector debt is denominated in terms of foreign currency (like most external debt), the debt becomes more costly when the domestic currency depreciates, making it more difficult for the borrowing country to repay the debt.

2. ELDCs which are dependent on the primary sector for exports are even more vulnerable to this, since primary commodities tend to be more price-volatile.

3. For example, copper accounts for at least 70% of Zambia's export revenues. From 2011 to 2020, world prices for copper gradually declined, causing

Zambia's copper export revenues to decline too.

4. Less demand for the Zambian kwacha by foreigners to buy Zambian copper exports caused the exchange rate to fall, with the kwacha gradually depreciating against the US dollar within the same period. This then made it more difficult for Zambia to repay its high external debt, culminating in the country defaulting on its US$12 billion external debt in 2020.

5. Additionally, ELDCs with high, unsustainable public sector debt may also resort to printing more money, increasing the money supply which lowers interest rates and leads to higher inflation. The high inflation then causes the real value of the debt to decrease, making it easier to repay.

6. However, excessively increasing the money supply leads to hyperinflation, as was the case in Zimbabwe where monthly inflation peaked at 79.6 billion % in 2008. Prices for basic goods & services (like bread and bus rides) skyrocketed in Zimbabwe especially since real output was not increasing, causing consumers' purchasing power and material welfare to fall drastically as the real value of their money drops and becomes worthless.

7. Both consumers and investors lost confidence in the Zimbabwean dollar (Z$), causing them to begin selling their holdings of Z$ and buying more stable foreign currencies such as US dollars (USD). Many consumers and producers switched to black markets where goods & services were sold in foreign currencies like USD.

8. As shown in Fig 3, demand (D) for the Z$ on the foreign exchange market fell from D_0 to D_1 while the supply (S) of Z$ in the market increased dramatically from S_0 to S_1. This then creates combined effect of the Z$ depreciating rapidly against USD from e_0 to e_1 as a result of the hyperinflation.

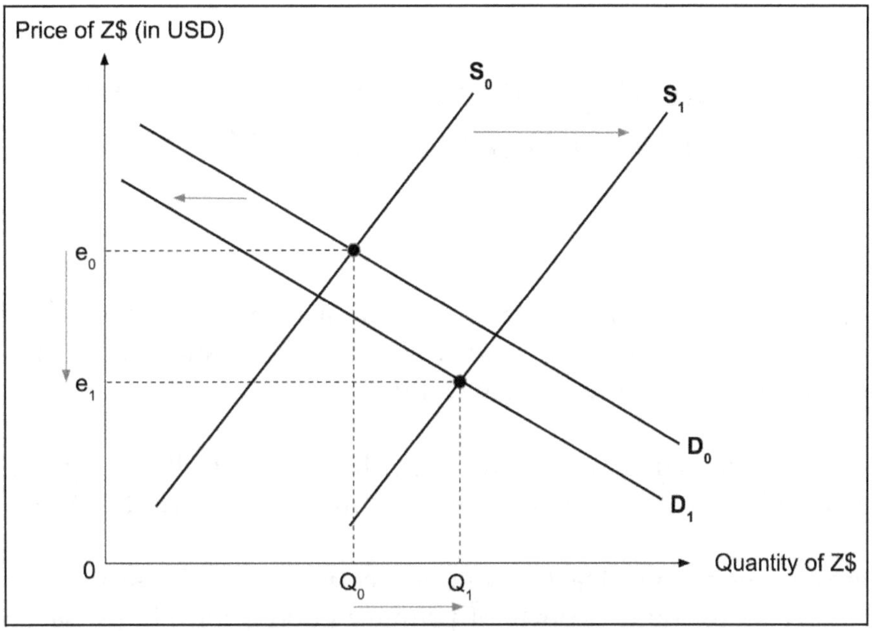

Fig 3: rapid depreciation of Z$ from hyperinflation

9. This then makes importing basic goods with Z$ even more difficult as one unit of Z$ can buy very little foreign currency, worsening shortages of such goods which then worsens the hyperinflation.

Concluding Section

1. Rising public sector debt may not necessarily be worrying if it is due to government spending to drive economic growth and development, although such effects may only be felt in the longer term.

2. However, public sector debt reaching unsustainable levels poses many challenges for low income countries in the short run, especially since these countries will struggle greatly to repay the debt.

3. Whether these low income countries will be able to reduce poverty and achieve economic development in the long run could ultimately depend on whether they are able to be fiscally sustainable and manage their debt well.

12. Explain how dependence on primary sector production may be a barrier to economic growth. (10)

Introduction

1. The primary sector of an economy includes industries involved in the extraction and production of raw materials, such as agriculture, fishing, forestry, and mining (e.g. oil and minerals).

2. Economic growth is the increase in the value of all final goods and services produced (or total output) by an economy over a period of time.

3. Many economically least developed countries (ELDCs) are dependent on the primary sector (and exports of primary goods) for a large part of its real gross domestic product (GDP). However, overspecialisation and dependence on the primary sector (and inability to diversify away from it) typically hinders prospects for economic growth.

4. This has led to the so-called "resource curse" where resource-rich ELDCs experienced much less economic growth compared to resource-poor countries.

Primary commodity exports tend to be price and output volatile

1. Demand for primary commodities tends to be more price-inelastic, and the Price Elasticity of Demand (PED) values for such goods tends to be relatively low ($PED < 1$).

2. This is because primary goods like agricultural products (e.g. food) and extracted products (e.g. coal, oil, minerals) tend to be necessities and lack readily available substitutes.

3. Additionally, the supply for primary commodities also tends to be price-inelastic, and their Price Elasticity of Supply (PES) values also tends to be relatively low ($PES < 1$).

4. This is because producers of primary goods cannot quickly change the quantity supplied in response to price changes. For agricultural goods, farmers need a long time (at least a planting season) to increase factor inputs like land and physical capital in response to an increase in price. Producers of oil and minerals require time to make the necessary investments in capital

goods before they can ramp up production in response to price increases.

5. Therefore, large changes in price results when there are demand and supply changes. Demand may change according to global economic conditions and supply may change for example due to weather shocks where agricultural markets are concerned.

6. As shown in Fig 1 below, changes in the supply of these goods (ceteris paribus), either increasing from S_0 to S_1 or decreasing from S_0 to S_2, results in a large change in the equilibrium price (*P*) between P_0 to P_1

7. As a result, for a given output produced, the ELDCs' export revenue earned would similarly fluctuate.

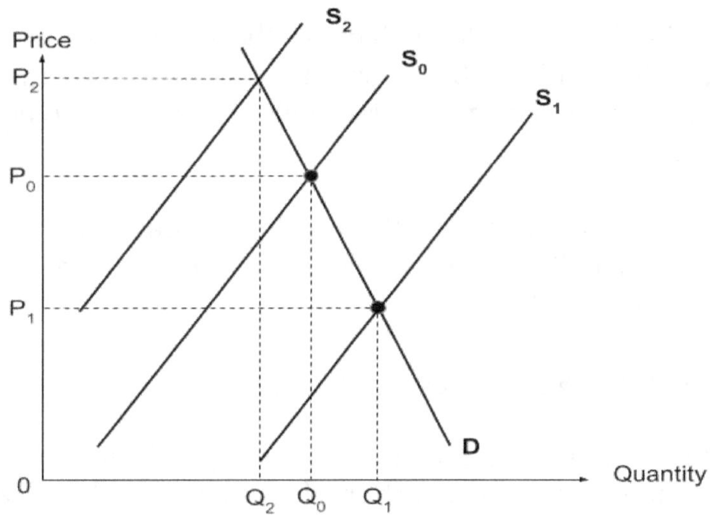

Fig 1: Price volatility due to Price-Inelasticity

8. Furthermore, agricultural goods are also more vulnerable to weather shocks, causing large changes in output.

9. Thus, TR earned by producers being volatile, investments and wages also become unstable, causing incomes earned to become unstable too.

10. Economic growth is then unstable as both investment spending (I) and export revenue (X) are unstable, and since both are components of real GDP, the real GDP will fluctuate greatly.

Demand for primary commodities globally is income-inelastic

1. Demand for primary goods tends to be income-inelastic, ie the YED value for these goods tends to be relatively low ($YED < 1$).

2. This is because, as mentioned, primary goods tend to be necessities. A 1% increase in income would then lead to a less-than-1% increase in the demand for goods like coal and agricultural products.

3. On the other hand, YED for higher value-added goods (like manufactured products) and services tend to be higher, with some even being luxury goods ($YED > 1$). Demand for such goods & services is therefore income-elastic; the same 1% increase in income would lead to a greater-than-1% increase in the demand.

4. For ELDCs highly dependent on the primary sector for exports, this would mean that with global economic growth over time, the demand for their primary commodity exports will increase relatively less than what they import.

5. Domestic economic growth may then be much slower compared to economic growth globally, widening the income disparity between the ELDCs and the rest of the world.

The primary sector is low-skilled and labour-intensive

1. In ELDCs, primary sectors such as agriculture may be labour-intensive and account for a large proportion of employment. However, such labour tends to be low-skilled.

2. Reliance on primary commodity exports for income could then possibly lead to a neglect of human capital, where spending on education and training are neglected as there may be no immediate need for it. Labour productivity then continues to be low.

3. There is also little investment in more advanced capital goods, which may require higher skill-sets. Adoption of such technologies could also be hindered for fears that they could displace workers and increase unemployment. Being low-tech hinders productivity and thus potential economic growth..

4. With productivity being low for the aforementioned reasons, the potential output of the economy cannot increase from Y_{f0} to Y_{f1} as shown in Fig 3 below. Real output, determined from where Aggregate Demand (AD) equals

Aggregate Supply (AS), is thus unable to increase from Y_0 to Y_1, showing how economic growth is thus limited.

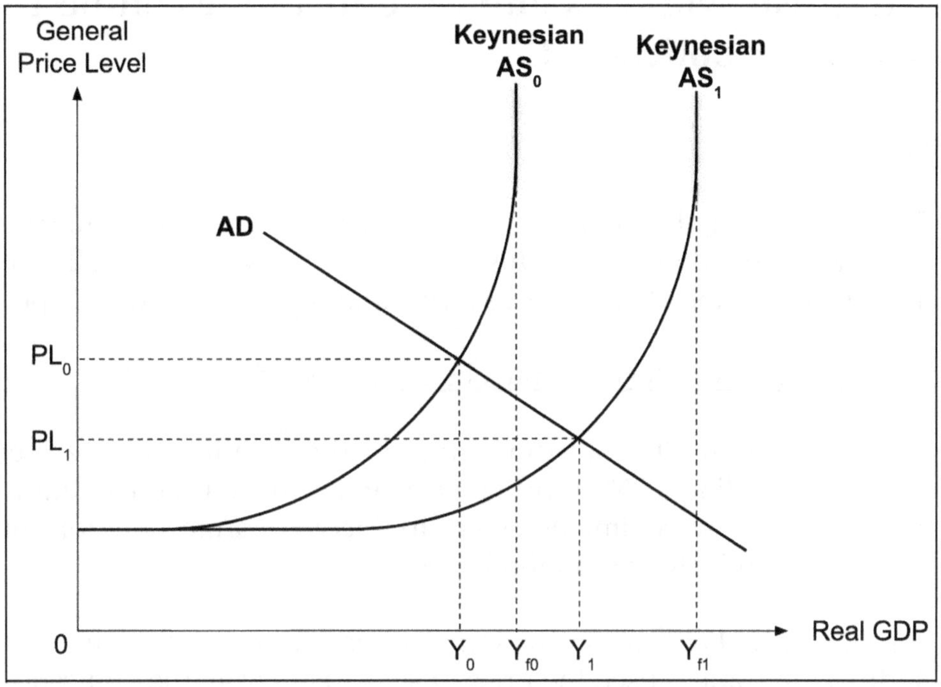

Fig 3: Economic growth hindered from primary sector dependence

13. Using real world examples, critically examine the use of protectionistic policies. (15)

Introduction

1. Protectionistic policies involve government intervention in international trade in favour of domestic industries over foreign. It usually involves the imposition of trade barriers, like tariffs and quotas, to reduce imports.

Argument 1: Domestic industries and jobs are protected

1. In 2018, under the Trump administration, the US implemented a set of "Trump tariffs", including a 25% tariff on steel and a 10% tariff on aluminium imports. Such policies were implemented to increase protection for the steel and aluminium industries from foreign competition.

2. As shown in Fig 1 below (using steel as an example), opening up the steel industry to trade caused the price of steel to fall from the domestic equilibrium P_{eqm} to the world price P_W. At this new price P_W, the quantity domestically supplied falls from Q_{eqm} to Q_S while the quantity demanded domestically increases from Q_{eqm} to Q_D. The quantity of steel imported then is $(Q_D - Q_S)$.

3. With this opening up to trade, domestic steel producers earn far less revenue as they are forced to produce at the lower world price P_W while also producing less at Q_S. The producer surplus, which is the difference between the price received by firms and the lowest price they are willing to accept for the good produced, also decreases greatly, shown in Fig 1 as the change from areas (b+d+h) to area h or alternatively a loss of areas (b+d).

4. The loss in revenue from being exposed to more low-cost and efficient global producers creates large job losses as firms are forced to cut costs to be able to compete and maintain profitability; some firms may even shut down from being unable to do so, which increases structural unemployment further.

5. The workers which are laid off and are unable to transition into other sectors due to lack of the right skills, could then fall into poverty as they remain unemployed.

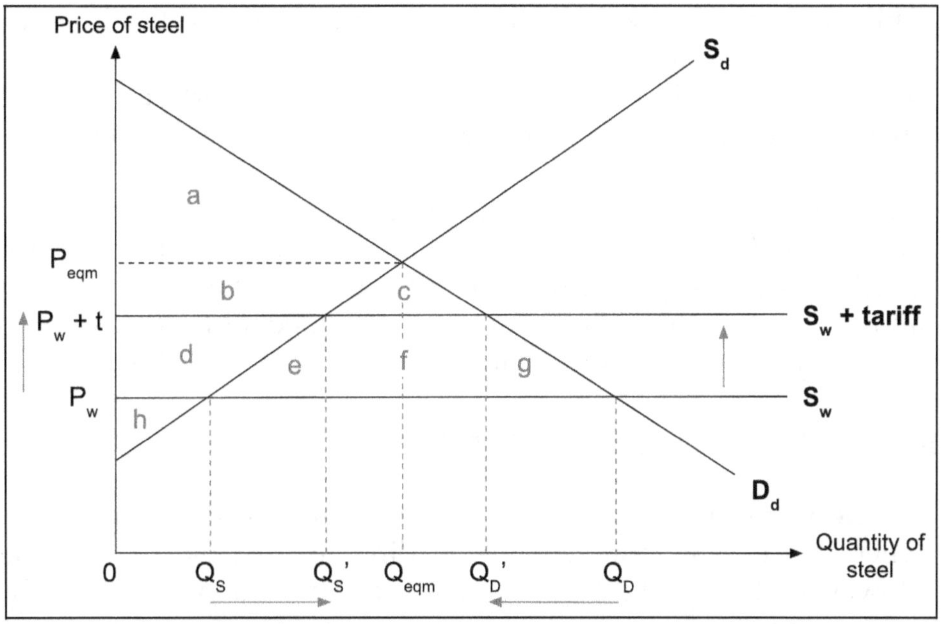

Fig 1: effect of tariff on steel (shown) and aluminium

6. With the imposition of the tariff, importers would then have to pay a higher price $(P_w + t)$ to import steel, making steel imports costlier. This becomes the new domestic price for steel, causing the domestic quantity demanded to fall from Q_D to Q_D' while the quantity supplied domestically increases from Q_S to Q_S'. The quantity of steel imported then falls from $(Q_D - Q_S)$ to $(Q_D' - Q_S')$.

7. With reduced competition from steel imports, the higher price received by domestic producers $(P_w + t)$ and increased production at Q_S' leads to higher revenues and improved profitability. Producers also gain back area d, with the producer surplus increasing from area h to areas (d+h).

8. Increased production also results in higher derived demand for labour, leading to higher employment in the US steel industry and several thousand jobs being protected. More workers are also then protected from structural unemployment and falling into poverty.

<u>Argument 2: Anti-dumping and national security concerns</u>

1. Both the US (under the aforementioned "Trump tariffs") and the UK (in 2022) have implemented tariffs on steel imports from China, with the UK also imposing import quotas. Such protectionist measures were also implemented as anti-dumping measures.

2. China has been accused of 'dumping', where its domestically produced steel is heavily subsidised by the government and produced at an artificially low cost before being sold on international markets. Exports of Chinese steel then creates unfair competition for steel producers in the US and the UK.

3. Furthermore, these protectionist policies were also implemented in the name of "national security" since steel is used for national defence, and thus considered a strategic sector by both the UK and the US. It would be unwise to allow the domestic steel sector to be wiped out by foreign competition, especially from a country that may be a likely military threat.

Argument 3: Infant industries and diversification

1. Developing economies may want to diversify away from the primary sector, where prices are more volatile leading to unstable revenues and growth. However, they might be unable to transition into producing more value-added, manufacturing goods due to fierce competition from global producers which prevents domestic producers from being profitable.

2. Mature competitors abroad, such as those in already developed economies, have had time to achieve economies of scale and lower average costs, thus being able to be highly competitive. Developing economies may therefore need to protect their newer infant industries from low-cost mature producers, giving them time to achieve economies of scale and productive efficiency so that they are able to compete with foriegn producers.

3. This is even more important if the developing country has potential to develop a comparative advantage in the good, but is unable to do so without some protection from foreign producers first.

4. South Korea – one of the Asian Tigers – historically achieved large economic growth rates and pulled off its "economic miracle" from protecting infant industries like car manufacturing.

5. Besides imposing tariffs on foreign-made cars, the Korean government passed legislation banning foreign automakers from operating in the country unless they were in joint ventures with local businesses. This significantly reduced competition from foreign automakers, allowing Korean automakers like Hyundai to expand, while also gaining technical expertise from mature foreign producers.

6. This allowed the Korean automotive industry to grow, and large exports of Korean-made cars helped contribute to strong export-led growth and diversification away from agriculture.

Counter-argument 1: Higher prices, which are passed onto consumers

1. Protectionistic policies, such as the Trump tariffs discussed earlier, reduce the competition faced by producers, thus reducing their incentive to cut costs. In addition, as inefficient domestic producers are protected, consumers face higher prices at $P_w + t$.
2. With the imposition of the Trump tariffs, the consumer surplus, which is the difference between the highest prices consumers are willing to pay for a good and the price actually paid, decreases significantly. This is shown in Fig 1 as the change from areas (a+b+c+d+e+f+g) before the tariff to areas (a+b+c) after the tariff; consumers lose areas (d+e+f+g).

3. Steel (and other goods covered under the Trump tariffs like aluminium, washing machines, and solar panels) directly become more expensive for consumers as now they have to pay a higher price ($P_w + t$). Consumers then consume less at Q_D'.

4. Furthermore, since aluminium and steel are used as inputs for other domestically manufactured goods like automobiles, the higher import costs for producers led to higher production costs and lower Short-Run Aggregate Supply (SRAS). As shown in Fig 2 below, this causes the SRAS curve to shift leftwards from $SRAS_0$ to $SRAS_1$, thus creating recessionary effects and cost-push inflation (ceteris paribus), shown by the real GDP decreasing from Y_0 to Y_1 while general price level increased from PL_0 to PL_1.

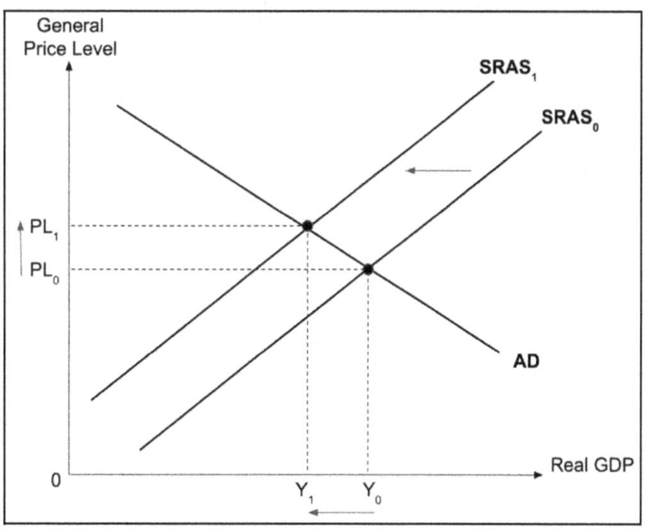

Fig 2: effect of higher production costs

5. After the tariffs were imposed, the consumer price index (CPI) for major household appliances and other tariffed goods increased dramatically. The average annual cost to American households due to the tariffs was estimated at US$414. The tariffs were also estimated to have caused the real national income to decline US$7.8 billion a year.

Counter-argument 2: Protectionist policies can worsen income distribution

1. Tariffs and quotas both cause consumer prices to increase, as explained earlier. This adversely affects lower-income groups more, especially if the tariffs or quotas cause the prices of necessities to increase.

2. For example, the Trump tariffs can be considered a kind of regressive tax, where lower-income groups spend a larger proportion of their income on the tariffs. Poorer Americans would have to spend an even greater proportion of their income on washing machines and other appliances.

3. The poor then have less income available for spending on healthcare and education. As shown in the poverty trap below (*Fig 3*), they will then have limited human capital which also limits their productivity, causing them to continue earning low incomes.

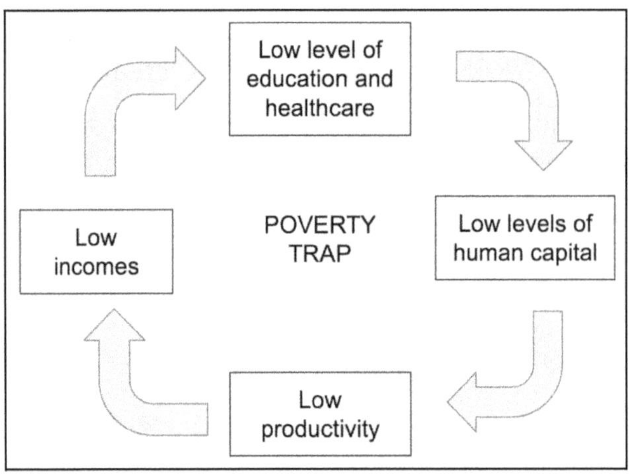

Fig 3: the poverty trap

4. It should be noted that these are happening whilst domestic producers are earning more revenue and thus profits as analused earlier. Thus, such protectionistic policies benefit the high income firm owners whilst hurting low income consumers..

Counter-argument 3: Retaliation by trading partners

1. Protectionist policies imposed by one country could lead to retaliatory protectionist policies being implemented by its trading partners. This was the case with the Trump tariffs and further tariffs set on imports from China by the US, which led to China setting their own trade barriers against US imports, ultimately escalating into a trade war.

2. The Trump administration had initially imposed the tariffs on US$550 billion of Chinese imports (like steel and aluminium) to try to reduce the US trade deficit. However, with China implementing tariffs on US$185 billion of US goods (including agricultural products) in response, the actual effect that the Trump tariffs had on the trade deficit became questionable.

3. The US-China trade war hurt American farmers in particular. The retaliation by China led to US agricultural exports to China significantly dropping from US$24 billion to US$9 billion. With much lower revenues, American farmers then faced a significant loss of income, causing many to make losses and face higher risk of falling into poverty.

4. US tariffs on Chinese imports as part of the trade war also resulted in a net loss in manufacturing jobs in the US. This is because, as explained earlier (*Counter-argument 1*), industries requiring the imported inputs, faced higher production costs which led to lower profit margins, resulting in firms cutting wages or laying off workers to reduce labour costs and maintain profitability.

5. The escalation into a trade war also hurt the Chinese economy, with the tariffs making Chinese exports to the US less competitive, causing industrial output to slow and resulting in an economic slowdown.

6. Retaliation and escalation into trade wars results in more inefficient domestic producers being protected from lower-cost foreign producers, resulting in a misallocation of global resources. Disruptions to global supply chains as a result of trade wars also result in imported inflationary pressures for countries that are not even involved in the trade war itself. Thus, there are many adverse repercussions from protectionistic policies.

Concluding Section

1. Whether protectionist policies bring about a net benefit to the economy is questionable. For example, in developed economies like the US, protectionistic policies may only benefit the protected industries while harming other producers (who face higher costs to import factor inputs) and consumers,

therefore having net negative effects on the economy.

2. On the other hand, developing economies may benefit greatly overall from protecting infant industries, which as explained earlier helps diversify the economy away from the primary sector, leading to higher incomes and stable economic growth.

3. It should be noted that arguments used by countries like "dumping" (which is difficult to prove) and "national security" are abusable and undermine the rules-based international trading system. Other forms of protectionism such as "hidden" protectionism, which includes administrative barriers, also hinder efforts to liberalise trade globally and lead to lower global economic growth and lesser improvement in standard of living.

4. Therefore, protectionistic policies are in general to be avoided. When used, they should be highly selective and only temporarily, for example to provide sufificent time for workers in declining sectors to learn new skills and for infant industries to grow up.

14. Explain how political and social factors can act as barriers to economic growth and economic development. (10)

Introduction

1. Economic growth can be defined as an increase in the real GDP of an economy over a period of time.

2. It can be categorised as either actual or potential economic growth, where actual growth is the annual percentage change in real GDP, caused by increases in aggregate demand (AD), and potential growth is the rate of increase in the economy's potential output.

3. Economic development is the sustained improvement in both material and non-material standards of living of residents in a country.

4. Material standard of living refers to the quantity and quality of goods & services available for consumption. Non-material standard of living refers to less tangible quality of life factors, such as education and health standards, environmental quality and the amount of leisure.

Political factors: Poor governance and corruption

1. Governance here refers to decision-making and implementation processes by the government for managing a country's resources to achieve both economic growth and development.

2. Corruption refers to the abuse of power for private gain, and includes bribery, embezzlement, graft, and extortion. Bribes, for example, to obtain a business licence can make investments costlier, therefore reducing investment spending (I) which reduces AD, limiting actual growth.

3. Corruption also leads to governmental funds being siphoned away and pocketed for personal use by government officials. Power asymmetry can also lead to political elites allocating resources and making decisions in a way that favours the interests of elite and wealthy groups, rather than benefitting society as a whole.

4. Funds are therefore not allocated to supporting the development process of a country, such as through financing infrastructure projects and provision of

merit goods.

5. The lack of infrastructure, education and healthcare therefore acts as a barrier to economic growth as poor infrastructure leads to slow or disrupted supply chains. Costs of production are higher just from transporting goods and services, which may not reach local or international markets, preventing firms from operating efficiently or profitably and deterring investments. The lack of healthcare and education provision also prevents the poor from escaping the poverty trap as seen below.

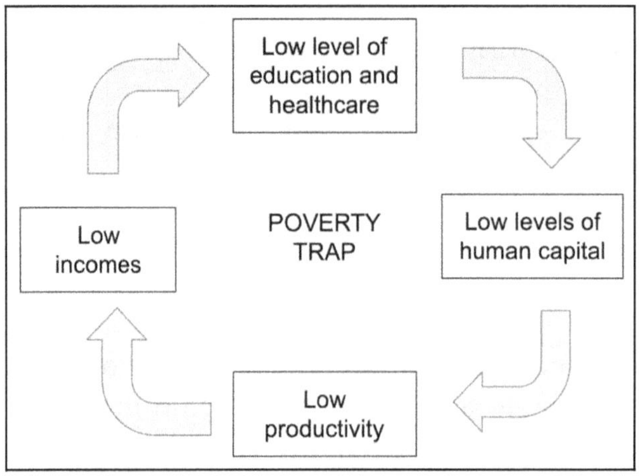

Fig 1: Poverty Trap

Social factors: Gender inequality

1. Cultural factors may limit girls' access to education as certain societies may view girls' education as less important compared to boys' education.

2. Limiting womens' access to educational attainment leads to their human capital being underdeveloped, limiting their productivity. There could also be gender discrimination within the labour market which prevents women from security stable and high-level jobs.

3. These both prevent women from fully developing and utilising their skills and talents, and these missed opportunities represent underemployment and unemployment of scarce labour resources. In countries with high gender inequality, this would mean that the economy is falling short of its potential output and producing far inside its production possibilities curve (PPC) (at point A in Fig 2), limiting the real output of the economy and acting as a barrier to actual growth.

4. It could also mean a lack of potential economic growth ie the PPC not shifting outwards by much, hence limiting long-term economic growth and

development.

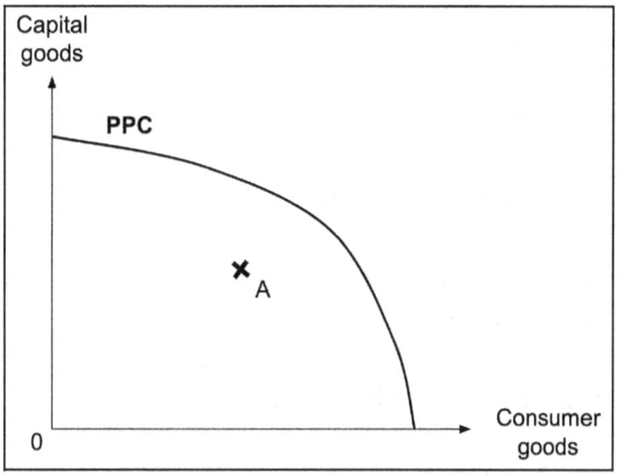

Fig 2: gender inequality leading to underemployment of labour

5. Less educated women typically result in higher child mortality as maternal knowledge on child health and nutrition is limited. This can also perpetuate the poverty and income inequality down the generations.

6. When more women are gainfully employed, birth rates will tend to be lower. This curbs population explosions in ELDCs and allows economic growth rates to exceed population growth rates, raising per capita incomes and thus the average person can enjoy more goods and services, raising material SOL.

<u>BONUS: Social factors: Inequalities of opportunity</u>

1. Different people living in the same society may not have access to the same opportunities, thus leading to differences in both incomes earned and outcomes.

2. Poorer people have less access to opportunities like education and healthcare compared to wealthier groups. Parental background, ethnicity, and (as explained) gender can also deny people access to these opportunities too.

3. With less access to education and healthcare, non-material standards of living and advancement of human capital will be limited, leaving them trapped in the poverty cycle.

4. Poor access to credit by banks also limits opportunities for small businesses and the poor. Small businesses cannot buy new capital goods, which hinders productivity and output. Poorer people continue to receive lesser human and physical capital.

5. If a significant portion of the population have such limited opportunities, lower labour productivity results in the potential output (Y_f) being unable to increase, thus hindering the potential economic growth shown in Fig 1. Low consumption expenditure (C) from low incomes and low investments (I) by businesses both limit AD and actual growth too.

6. For these disadvantaged groups, low incomes and a lack of education and healthcare then also hinders the opportunities available to their children, for reasons like lower spending on their children's education and higher child mortality. The cycle of inequality is thus perpetuated and upward social mobility is restricted. Low material and non-material standards of living will persist, thus impeding development.

15. Using real world examples, discuss the view that weak institutional framework in ELDCs represents the most significant barrier to economic growth. (15)

Introduction

1. Economic growth is the increase in real GDP of an economy over a period of time. Growth can be divided into actual growth which is the annual percentage change in real GDP, and potential growth which is the rate of increase in full employment output.

2. The weak institutional framework in many economically least developed countries (ELDCs) represents a significant barrier to economic growth. Various aspects of the institutional framework, such as a poorly-functioning legal system, ineffective/inequitable taxation structure, underdeveloped banking system, and lack of property rights, can act as impediments to economic growth.

Thesis 1: Weak Legal System and Lack of Property Rights

1. Property rights are essential for economic growth as they provide individuals and businesses with the security to invest in and develop assets. Without clear property rights, individuals may hesitate to invest in property or engage in productive activities. This also hinders the possibility to use assets as collateral to access loans to invest in productive resources.

2. Haiti, for example, has struggled with unclear property rights, leading to many disputes and challenges in property ownership.

3. In addition, a weak legal system where contracts may be unenforceable, property rights may not be protected, and disputes may go unresolved has severely hampered Haiti's economic growth.

4. All such uncertainties and risks discourage domestic and foreign investment as well as hamper domestic entrepreneurship. As a result, investments (I) remain dampened, and Aggregate Demand (AD) thus remains low, resulting in lack of actual economic growth.

5. As investments (I) consist of adding capital goods to the economy and entrepreneurship is a factor of production, this also means that the Aggregate Supply (AS) remains low, with a lack of potential economic growth.

6. Even where substantial property and assets are available, without property rights and a strong legal system, the people are hindered from utilising and enhancing their assets to improve their wellbeing.

Thesis 2: Ineffective Taxation Systems

1. It is difficult for governments of ELDCs to collect substantial income tax revenue since there are low incomes. In addition, foreign firms are often given tax concessions to attract their investments. Moreover,a significant number of workers may be working informally, which is unrecorded or unreported work, and thus without payment of taxes.

2. Corruption in tax collection will also divert resources away from being productively used, and together with an inefficient tax system, insufficient tax revenues are earned.

3. The government then lacks funds to improve the supply-side of the economy, such as in areas of infrastructure, healthcare and education, which leads to a lack of potential economic growth. Actual economic growth is also hindered due to a lack of investments (I) since productivity would be low.

4. This is certainly true for the Democratic Republic of Congo, which has faced such challenges of an ineffective tax structure and corruption, which hampered revenue collection and hindered public investments needed for economic growth.

Thesis 3: Banking and access to credit

1. Finally, an underdeveloped banking system (such as in Mozambique) has caused limited access to credit and financing for businesses and individuals.

2. When they are weak and untrustworthy financial institutions, people do not save in these institutions and that causes a lack of credit. At the same time borrowing would be difficult and at very high interest rates.

3. Thus, there is little opportunity to accumulate funds through earning a return on savings and also difficulty in borrowing. This would limit spending on human capital such as on healthcare and education, investments (I), innovation and entrepreneurship, constraining both actual and potential economic growth..

Weak institutional frameworks acting as a barrier to growth

1. Thus, it can be said that strong instructional frameworks are like a foundation for weak institutional frameworks clearly constrain economic growth with AD and AS being unable to increase, stuck at AD_0 and AS_0 as seen in the Fig 1 below, compared to a case of strong institutional frameworks that would lead to sustained growth from Y_0 to Y_1.

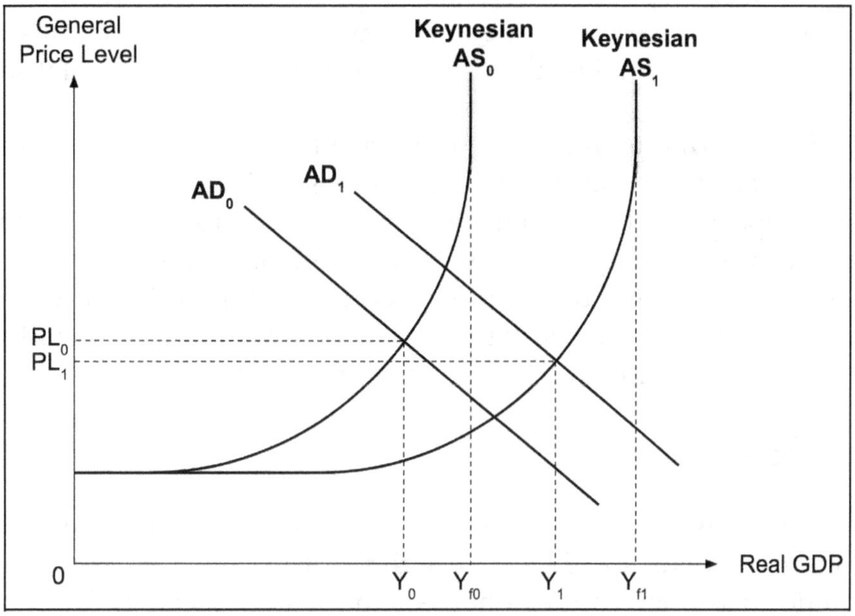

Fig 1: weak institutional frameworks hinder growth

Antithesis 1: Political instability and conflict could be more significant

1. However, while the weak institutional framework is a significant barrier to economic growth in many ELDCs, it may not always be the most significant barrier.

2. In some ELDCs, political instability and conflict can overshadow the impact of weak institutions. Persistent conflict can disrupt economic activities, destroy infrastructure, and displace populations, creating an environment where even well-functioning institutions would struggle to promote growth.

3. For example, South Sudan, which gained independence in 2011, has faced persistent conflict and political instability. These factors have hindered both economic growth more than weak institutions.

Antithesis 2: External factors are significant too

1. Economic growth in ELDCs can also be heavily influenced by external factors, such as global commodity prices and trade policies of developed countries.. Weak institutions within ELDCs may not be as influential when external factors are unfavourable.

2. For example, ELDCs heavily reliant on a single commodity export, like Zambia with copper exports and Angola with oil, can experience economic fluctuations driven by global commodity prices. Weak institutions, while problematic, may not be the primary driver of economic volatility.

3. In addition, due to subsidies and price floors that the European Union (EU) government implement to boost incomes of its farmers, it not only closes up the european market for farmers in african nations like Mozambique, it also leads to them being unable to sell to neighbouring african countries as the surpluses from agricultual price floors are dumped onto overseas markets. Such circumstances heavily prevent economic growth of the ELDCs regardless of whether weak institutional frameworks exist.

Concluding Section

1. While a weak institutional framework is undoubtedly a significant barrier to economic growth in ELDCs, it is difficult to conclude whether it is the most significant barrier as the other economic and social or political barriers can also be very significant and it is essential to consider the multifaceted and inter-related nature of development challenges.

2. Addressing institutional weaknesses is a crucial step, but a comprehensive approach that also tackles other barriers is necessary to promote sustainable economic growth in these countries.

16. Countries often specialise and trade according to the theory of comparative advantage. Explain the limitations of this approach. (10)

Introduction

1. A country that has comparative advantage (CA) in the production of a good is one that is able to produce the good at a lower opportunity cost compared to another country.

2. A country should specialise in the production of goods that it has CA in, and export them, while importing goods it does not have CA in. As long as opportunity costs in 2 or more countries differ, it is possible for countries to gain from specialisation and trade according to their CA. This will improve efficiency in the global allocation of resources, resulting in greater global output and allowing countries to consume outside their production possibility curves (PPCs).

Assumptions made in the theory of CA are not realistic

1. However, there are several limitations to the theory of CA as its assumptions are not realistic. Firstly, resources are assumed to be homogeneous, with perfect occupational mobility and thus constant opportunity cost.

2. This is clearly untrue in reality. The same labour and machine cannot produce different goods or cannot produce them as efficiently. Therefore, specialisations according to comparative advantage may be limited by this issue as when the economy deploys more and more of its resources to produce a good, higher and higher opportunity costs may be incurred till it would make more sense for the economy to produce alternative goods instead.

3. In addition, the theory assumes zero transportation costs. However, this is not the case in the real world, and some countries may not engage in trade even with cheaper imports, due to prohibitively high transportation costs over long geographic distances between countries. Thus, it may result in difficulty exporting the goods they have CA in and importing those they lack CA in. Higher costs may end up having to be incurred to import goods the country does not have CA in. This is also why alot of trade typically happens between neighbouring countries, even though some other faraway country may actually produce the goods at lower opportunity cost.

4. The theory of CA also relies on the assumption that countries are able to specialise and trade freely without any form of trade barriers such as tariffs or import quotas. This is unrealistic, as in the real world, there is protectionism to protect domestic industries.

5. Thus, if countries specialise in accordance with their CA, they may find themselves unable to export all the goods they produce and due to a lack of export earnings and foreign exchange or even trade barriers, unable to import enough of goods they do not produce. This would eventually cause specialisation and trade in accordance to CA to be unviable.

<u>Specialisation does not allow necessary structural changes to occur</u>

1. Furthermore, specialisations may not allow necessary structural changes to occur in an economy. These structural changes are important for developing countries, indicating that CA is dynamic. For example, a country may have comparative advantage in agricultural production initially, but over time, it may stand a chance to acquire comparative advantage in manufactured goods instead, due to increased physical capital and more educated workforce.

2. If countries always specialise according to their comparative advantage, they would have to continue producing that same good, which will not permit necessary structural changes to occur in the economy. It would be better for countries to diversify their export industries from simply agricultural products, as diversification will result in higher-value added production, such as shifting from exporting raw cocoa beans to refining cocoa beans into chocolate bars to be sold.

3. Diversification will protect countries from over-dependence on a singular type of export. For example, if there is a fall in demand for cocoa beans due to a global recession, there will be a fall in export revenues, falling incomes and economic decline. However, these negative effects will be mitigated if a country has diversified its export industry into chocolate manufacturing.

17. Discuss whether maintaining a healthy balance of trade takes priority over other macro objectives. (15)

Introduction

1. The Balance of Trade (BOT) is the total export revenue (X) minus the total import expenditure (M) for currently produced goods & services over a period of time.

2. A healthy BOT can be defined as having no persistent deficits and no persistent surpluses. In reality, most ecomomies would prefer a net zero or surpluses.

3. Other macro objectives are sustainable and inclusive economic growth, full employment and price stability.

Thesis 1: Accumulation of foreign exchange reserves

1. Maintaining a healthy BOT should take priority because it can allow for an accumulation of Foreign Exchange Reserves. For example, if there are occasional BOT surpluses, meaning Export Revenue exceeds Import Expenditure ($X_{rev} > M_{exp}$), then there is net inflow of currency into the economy, which can be added into the foreign exchange reserves held by the central bank.

2. There are a few benefits of this such as allowing the central bank to have foreign currencies to implement exchange rate policies. For example, to appreciate the currency, the central bank has to sell foreign currency in the Forex Market to buy domestic currency.

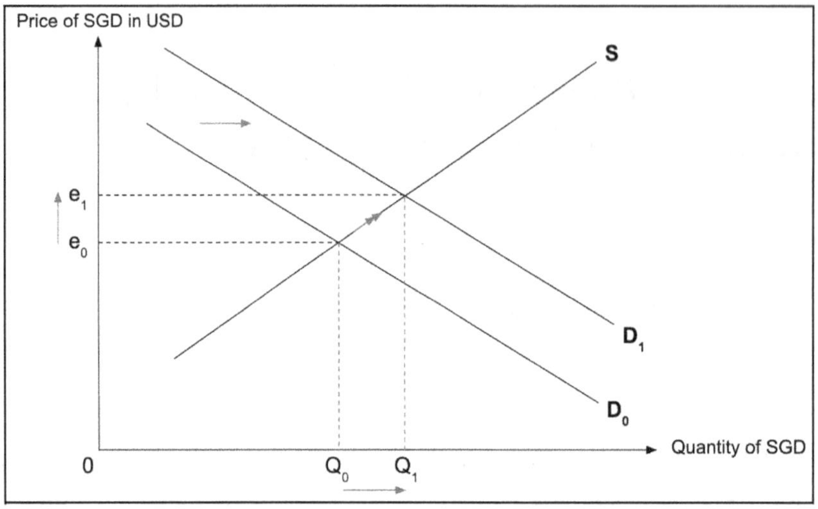

Fig 1: currency appreciation from selling foreign reserves

3. As shown in Fig 1 above, this would increase demand for the domestic currency from D_0 to D_1, thus causing the value of the domestic currency to increase from e_0 to e_1, bringing out the appreciation.

4. Having Forex Reserves will also help secure the economy's ability to afford imports into the future; this can help secure future standard of living as well as critical factor inputs for production.

Thesis 2: A healthy BOT is an indicator of economic competitiveness

1. A healthy balance of trade can also be a good indicator of economic competitiveness, which is a key determinant of long-term economic growth.

2. Take the example of Ireland from 2000 to 2007. High economic growth rates, full employment and price stability were all achieved during this time frame. However it was experiencing a rapidly increasing BOT deficits — clearly a sign of something wrong with its economy, and because the government did not take heed, eventually its economy crashed in 2008.

3. The reason why Ireland was experiencing rapidly increasing trade deficits was due to a lack of competitiveness causing export revenues (X_{rev}) to be falling whilst import expenditure (M_{exp}) was increasing. Its economy was still growing due to a housing and construction boom but that is not a sustainable source of economic growth. Failure to prioritise maintaining a healthy balance of trade eventually led Ireland to economic downfall.

Antithesis 1: Inflationary pressures

1. However, there are also a few reasons why maintaining a healthy balance of trade should not take priority. For example, if the economy is already near or at full employment (Y_{fe}), prioritising a healthy balance of trade may lead to increasing net exports (X–M) which would increase aggregate demand from AD_0 to AD_1, leading to high demand-pull inflation as shown in Fig 2 by the general price level increasing greatly from PL_0 to PL_1.

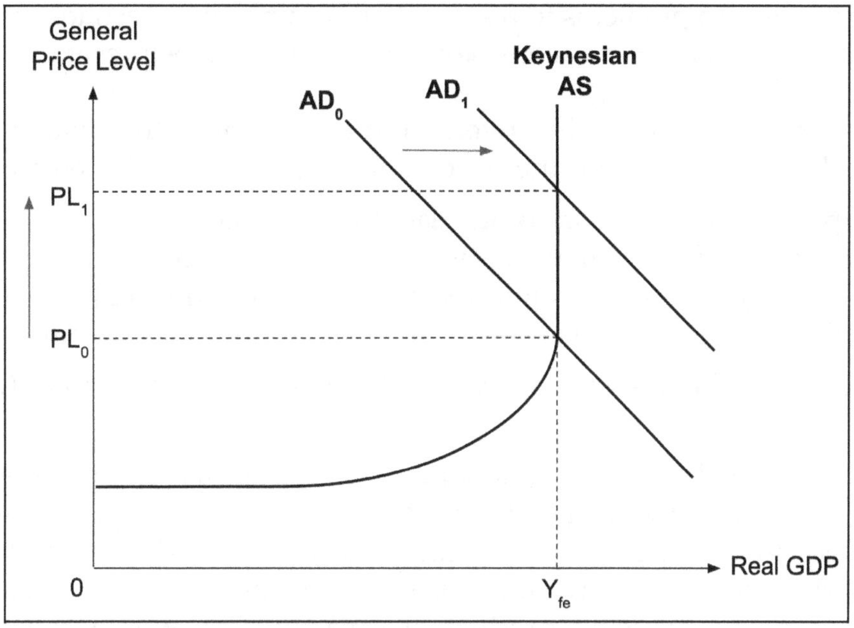

Fig 2: high demand-pull inflation

2. This will in turn cause business uncertainty, which may reduce investments and derail economic growth. It can also cause standard of living to fall especially for the fixed income earners, who will experience a fall in real incomes.

Antithesis 2: A trade surplus in one country corresponds to trade deficits in other countries, leading to retaliation

1. Prioritising a healthy BOT may also cause the government to be pursuing surpluses which can cause trading partners to be experiencing persistent trade deficits.

2. In such a scenario, trading partners may end up experiencing the negative effects of persistent trade deficits and retaliate against this economy. A case in point is the US-China trade relations with China persistently experiencing a

trade surplus and the US persistently in trade deficit.

3. This led to the US imposing trade barriers against China since 2018, which does not benefit China since this would mean less Chinese exports to the US, reducing China's aggregate demand and thus economic growth and employment as well.

<u>Antithesis 3: There could be more urgent macro problems to handle</u>

1. Achieving other macro objectives may take priority as that could be more urgent macro problems to resolve. For example, if the economy is experiencing a recession then rising unemployment would also be present.

2. In such a scenario, if the government were to prioritise maintaining a healthy BOT (and view that the recession is positive as it reduces M_{exp}, which improves the BOT), it could lead to a deeper recession as household and business confidence may continue to worsen given that the government is not actively pursuing economic recovery. Consumption (C) and investments (I) will continue to decrease, causing AD to fall further from AD_1 to AD_2 and worsening the recession as real GDP falls further from Y_1 to Y_2 (Fig 3).

3. This can lead to massive and long-term unemployment resulting in drastic fall in standard of living and also adverse long-term consequences to the economy as long-term unemployment can lead to loss of skills and the discouraged worker effect which would cause a fall in the quality and quantity of labour respectively, reducing productive capacity. This would cause the potential output of the economy to fall from Y_{f0} to Y_{f1} (Fig 3).

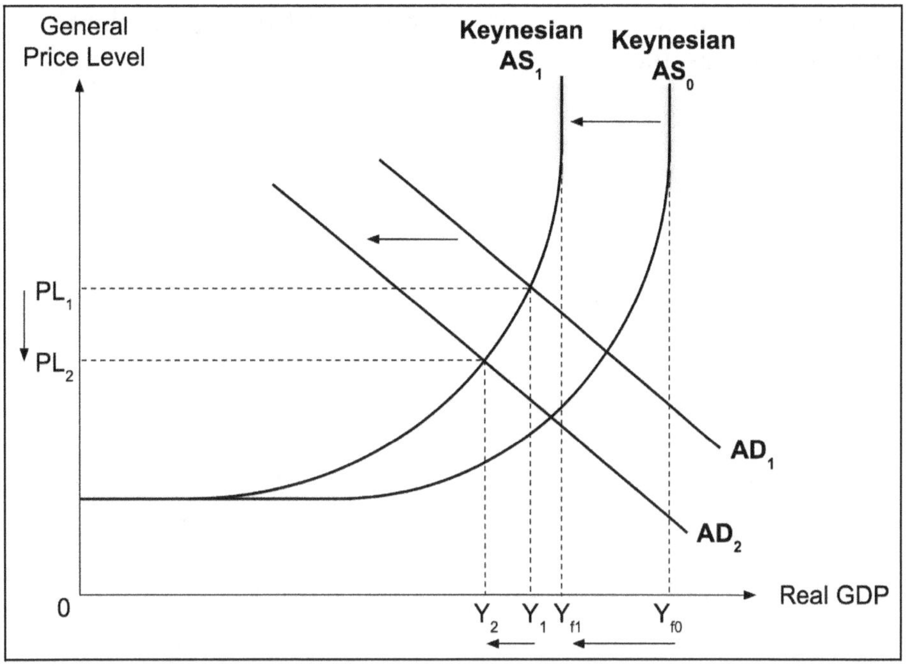

Fig 3: worsening recession and long-term negative potential growth

4. And even in the case of high inflation, if the government is not prioritising tackling the high inflation, it can easily result in inflationary spirals and hyperinflation as seen in countries like Zimbabwe and Venezuela, which literally leads to the collapse of the currency and the economy.

5. For example, with high inflation, labour unions may be fighting for higher wages in order to maintain real wages. Should they succeed, it will lead to higher cost of production which in turn will fuel the inflation causing a wage-price spiral, which may result in hyperinflation.

Concluding Section

1. In conclusion, I would say that maintaining a healthy BOT should usually not take priority over other macro goals.

2. This is because a lack of economic growth, high unemployment and price instability usually brings about even more significant and immediate adverse effects on standard of living than balance of trade issues. Therefore, very often, other macro objectives may have to take priority.

3. It also does depend on the nature of the economy. The more trade-dependent an economy is (e.g. Singapore), then the more important it is to maintain a healthy BOT. This is because it will have a more direct and very significant

effect on economic growth, employment and living standards as compared to large economies like the US.

18. Explain what is meant by a favourable balance of trade (BOT) / balance of payments (BOP). (10)

Introduction

1. The Balance of Payments (BOP) of a country is a record of all transactions between the residents of the country and residents of all other countries, showing payments received and made to other countries.

2. The BOP consists of several accounts. The current account (CA) is the sum of the balance of trade in goods and services, net income flows and current transfers. The capital account (KA) shows net capital flows for capital transfers and transactions in non-produced, non-financial assets. The financial account (FA) consists of net flows of funds for direct investments and financial investments.

3. For most economies, attaining a healthy BOP is an important objective. A healthy BOP can be defined as achieving a net zero equilibrium in the long-run. Persistent surpluses and deficits are typically a cause of concern as they have detrimental effects on the economy.

Consequences of a persistent BOP deficit

1. When a country has a persistent BOP deficit, that means that their international outflows to other countries are greater than the international inflows.

2. For one, a persistent deficit can cause the depletion of foreign exchange (forex) reserves. This would, in turn, limit the government's ability to enact certain economic policies, such as exchange rate interventions. With a lack of foreign reserves, the government is unable to purchase domestic currency from the Forex market, and thus its ability to appreciate or maintain its currency value is limited.

3. This also leaves the economy exposed and vulnerable to speculative attacks. This was the case during the Asian Financial Crisis in 1997, where Thailand had to bear the brunt of such speculative attacks where speculators sold their holdings of the Thai Baht, causing the supply of Baht on the Forex market to increase from S_0 to S_1, devaluing the Baht from e_{fixed} to e_1.

4. With a lack of foreign reserves, it was unable to 'defend' against such attacks by purchasing the excess quantities of Baht on the forex market by increasing demand for the Baht from D_0 to D_1. As a result, the Thai Baht became highly unstable, which in turn deterred trade and also put off investment inflows into Thailand, harming its economy.

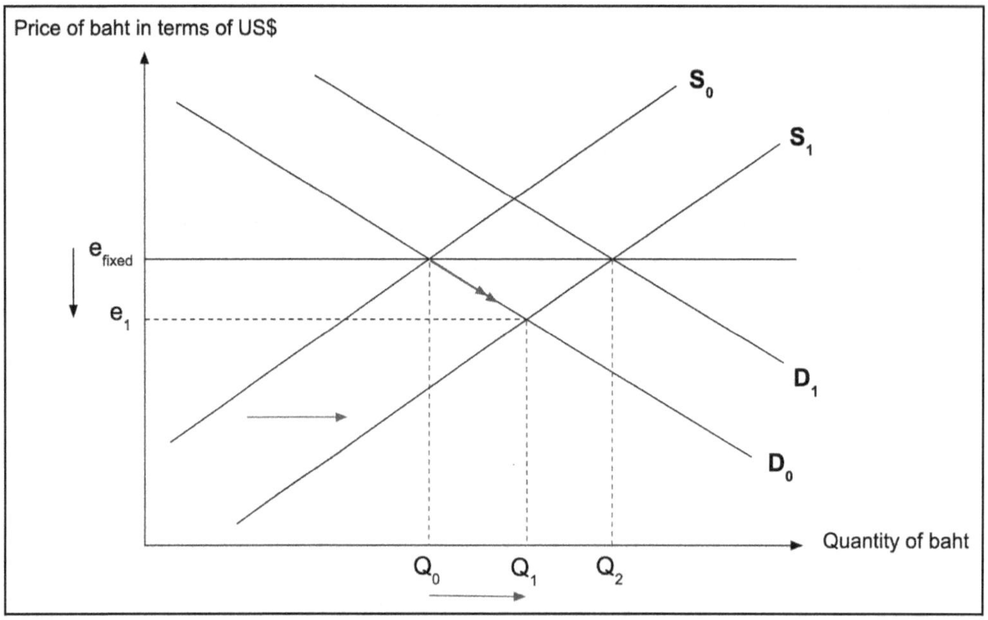

Fig 1: Low forex reserves preventing Thailand from defending Baht

5. A lack of foreign reserves would also cause the country to be unable to finance purchase of imports, which may include basic necessities like food. This would have severe consequences on the standard of living of citizens. It can also mean the inability to import certain factors of production and that can also cause economic production and employment to decline.

<u>Consequences of a persistent BOP surplus</u>

1. A persistent BOP surplus, on the other hand, indicates that a country's international inflows are greater than its international outflows to other countries.

2. Persistent BOP surpluses may lead to animosity between countries, and the threat of retaliatory action. This is because the surplus could indicate a lopsided relationship between trading partners, whereby other countries face persistent deficits in the BOT and BOP.

3. For instance, the trade war between the US and China emerged due to the US$ 336 billion trade deficit between the two trading partners. The US imposed

tariffs and other trade barriers on China and vice-versa, reducing the price-competitiveness of Chinese and American exports, thereby reducing both countries' export revenue. In addition, China has also lost out on alot of investments as firms relocated or expanded its operations in other countries like Vietnam that are not affected by the US tariffs. The trade war has greatly slowed down China's economy.

4. A persistent BOP surplus could also lead to an exchange rate appreciation of the domestic currency. For example, short-term capital inflows would necessarily entail an increased demand for the domestic currency on the forex market, thereby causing appreciation.

5. This would negatively impact export-oriented economies, as a strong exchange rate would make exports relatively more expensive to other countries, while making imports relatively cheaper to locals. This can have the effect of decreasing net export revenue, which could impede economic growth and increase unemployment.

6. A BOP surplus may also lead to the overheating of the economy. A persistent surplus suggests a stream of net inflows of funds, that expand the money supply of a country and places a downward pressure on interest rates thereby leading to increases in the consumption (C) and investment (I) components of aggregate demand (AD). Together with increasing net exports and foreign direct investments (FDI), this could lead to AD increasing (from AD_0 to AD_1 in Fig 2) in excess of AS, resulting in high demand-pull inflation and its detrimental consequences.

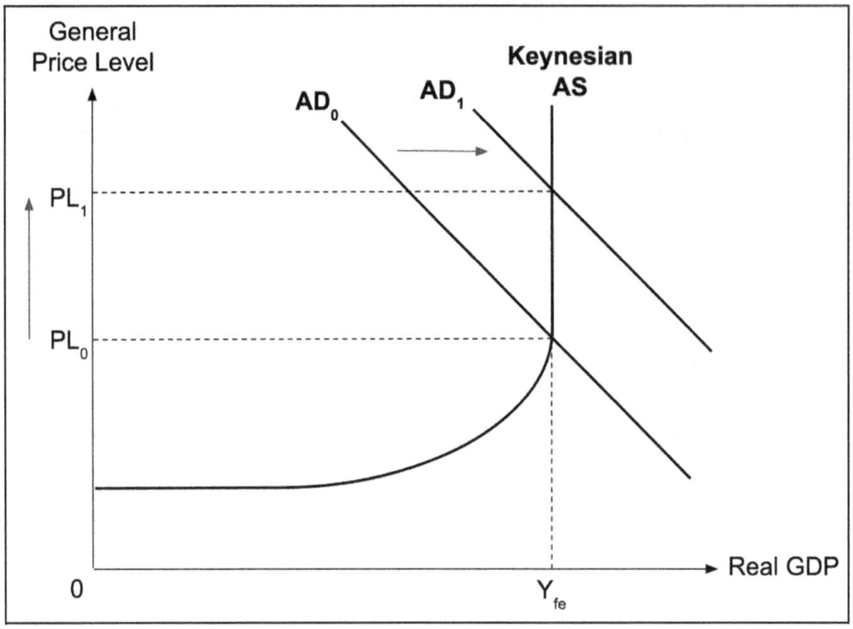

Fig 2: high demand-pull inflation

7. However, exceptions exist. Small and open economies that lack natural resources, such as Singapore, are naturally trade-dependent, and FDI-dependent. It is thus in such countries' advantage to have a persistent BOP surplus, which indicates a high level of exports and FDI that drives economic growth, while allowing an accumulation of foreign reserves to conduct exchange rate interventions and finance imports. Adverse consequences of a persistent surplus are also somewhat mitigated for small and open economies, as due to their smallness in size, it is unlikely to be a cause of significant trade or BOP deficits in other countries.

19. Assess the role of international organisations such as the IMF and the World Bank in promoting economic development in low-income countries. (15)

Introduction

1. Economic development is the sustained improvement in both material and non-material economic well-being of residents in a country.

2. Material well-being refers to the quantity and quality of goods & services available for consumption to consumers. Non-material well-being refers to less tangible quality of life factors, such as education and health standards, gender equality, and environmental quality.

3. International organisations like the International Monetary Fund (IMF) and the World Bank play a significant role in promoting economic development in low-income countries. These institutions provide financial assistance, technical expertise, and policy advice to struggling economies.

Argument 1: Financial assistance

1. From an economic perspective, financial assistance from international organisations like the IMF and the World Bank can help low-income countries overcome balance of payments (BOP) problems and fiscal deficits. This is particularly crucial when countries face external shocks or economic crises, as it can prevent a downward spiral.

2. For example, in the 1990s, Mexico experienced a severe financial crisis. The IMF provided a financial package to stabilise its currency and restore investor confidence. This assistance helped Mexico avoid a full-blown economic meltdown and contributed to its subsequent economic recovery.

Argument 2: Technical expertise

1. Economically, the technical expertise offered by these organisations can lead to better policy formulation and implementation. By aligning economic policies with international best practices, countries can enhance their competitiveness and attract foreign investment.

2. India's economic reforms in the early 1990s, with guidance from the World Bank and the IMF, led to liberalisation, privatisation, and globalisation. These

reforms improved India's economic performance and contributed to its emergence as a major global economy.

Argument 3: Capacity-building

1. Economically, capacity-building programs can enhance a country's productive capacity and administrative efficiency, leading to higher economic growth rates. Strengthened institutions can reduce corruption, improve regulatory environments, and attract foreign investment.

2. For example, the World Bank has supported education initiatives in Kenya, including funding for the Free Primary Education program. This program aimed to increase access to education for children in low-income households.

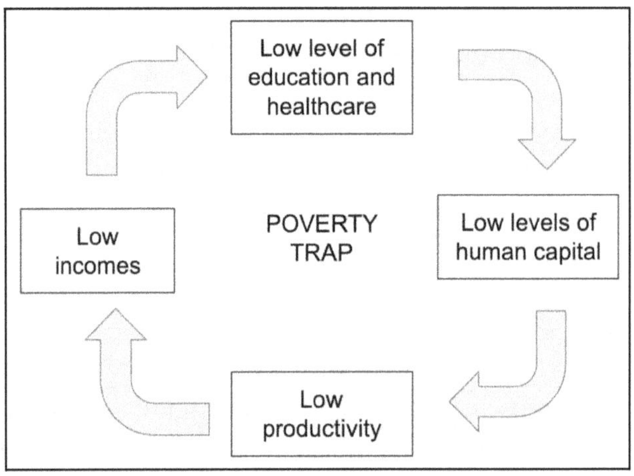

Fig 1: the poverty trap

3. Thus, the World Bank contributed to human capital development, which improved these children's productivity once they entered the workforce and allowed them to earn higher incomes. More people are able to escape the poverty trap shown in Fig 1, increasing both material and non-material well-being, leading to development.

4. Higher labour productivity also results in the full-employment output of the economy increasing, leading to potential economic growth too.

Argument 4: Policy reform

1. Both the IMF and the World Bank impose conditions when providing financial assistance to countries. From an economic standpoint, conditionalities imposed by these international organisations can address structural weaknesses and macroeconomic imbalances. These conditions often focus on fiscal discipline, monetary stability, and trade liberalisation, which are

essential for long-term economic development.

2. Post-Soviet countries like Estonia and Latvia implemented structural reforms and austerity measures as part of their IMF programs in the early 1990s. These reforms paved the way for rapid economic growth and integration into the European Union.

3. While these conditions may be viewed as intrusive, they often serve to create fiscal discipline and improve economic policies. They can also help combat corruption, a pervasive issue in many low-income countries that hinders economic growth. By addressing corruption, more resources can be directed towards essential services like healthcare and education, which are vital for human development.

<u>Counter-argument 1: The policy reforms imposed by the IMF or the World Bank may be inappropriate</u>

1. For example, Argentina has a history of seeking IMF assistance during economic crises. In 2018, the country entered into a $57 billion IMF program aimed at stabilising its economy. The IMF's conditions included fiscal austerity measures. While the program aimed to address Argentina's fiscal issues, critics argue that these policies contributed to recession and social unrest, highlighting the social impact of IMF conditions.

2. During Greece's debt crisis, the IMF, along with other creditors, imposed austerity measures as conditions for financial assistance. These measures included cuts to public spending and tax increases. While these policies aimed to address fiscal deficits, they resulted in social protests and economic hardship for many Greeks, exemplifying the social impact and political challenges associated with IMF programs. Many Greeks felt that these decisions were made without their input or consent, leading to protests and a sense of democratic deficit in the decision-making process.

3. Some African countries have experienced difficulties in promoting export-led growth due to IMF conditions favouring stable exchange rates. Ethiopia, for instance, chose to maintain a fixed exchange rate for years under IMF guidance, which some argue hindered the country's competitiveness and export potential in the long term.

4. In the late 1990s, Russia implemented market-oriented reforms and liberalisation policies as part of an IMF program. Critics argue that these policies contributed to economic instability and wealth inequality, and they did not necessarily align with the country's long-term development goals. The rapid privatisation of key industries led to the emergence of powerful

monopolies in sectors such as natural resources, media, and telecommunications. This concentration of power and limited competition had negative consequences for consumers and economic competition. It also increased income inequality.

5. Zambia's experience with IMF-imposed conditions in the early 2000s raised questions about sovereignty. The IMF urged the Zambian government to privatise state-owned enterprises as a condition for financial assistance. Critics argued that this undermined the government's ability to control key sectors of its economy.

Counter-argument 2: Social and environmental concerns

1. From an economic perspective, addressing social and environmental concerns is essential for sustainable development. Neglecting these issues can result in long-term economic costs, such as healthcare expenses and environmental damage.

2. The controversy surrounding the Chad-Cameroon Oil Pipeline, funded by the World Bank, highlighted the need to balance economic development with environmental and social considerations. Proponents argued that the project would boost economic growth, while critics raised concerns about its environmental impact and impact on local communities.

Counter-argument 3: Excessive borrowing to fund the required reforms

1. Countries that rely heavily on loans from international financial institutions may face interest rate risk. If global interest rates rise, the cost of servicing debt increases, potentially leading to fiscal strain and debt sustainability issues.

2. Borrowing from the IMF and World Bank can also indirectly contribute to such debt problems, even if the borrowing is offered at favourable terms.

Concluding Section

1. In conclusion, international organisations like the IMF and the World Bank play multifaceted roles in promoting economic development in low-income countries. While they provide crucial financial support, their impact extends beyond financial assistance, encompassing policy advice, project financing, and efforts to address systemic issues like corruption and inequality. However, it is imperative that these organisations continue to adapt their strategies to the evolving needs and challenges faced by developing nations.

2. The effectiveness and impact of their programs depend on various factors, including the specific conditions, the implementation of reforms, and the country's ability to manage its finances effectively.

3. Careful consideration and close monitoring of the debt situation are essential to avoid unsustainable debt burdens in the long run. Debt relief initiatives are sometimes necessary to alleviate the burden on heavily indebted countries.

20. Explain two reasons why a high level of government indebtedness can act as a barrier to economic growth. (10)

Introduction

1. Economic growth can be defined as an increase in the real GDP of an economy over a period of time.

2. It can be in terms of either actual or potential economic growth, where actual growth is the annual percentage change in real GDP, while potential growth which is the annual percentage change in the economy's full employment output level.

Reason 1: Higher taxes and reduced government spending

1. To manage their debt obligations, governments may resort to increasing taxes and/or reducing public spending in various sectors.

2. Higher taxes can reduce consumers' disposable income, leading to decreased consumer spending, and since consumer expenditure (C) is a component of Aggregate Demand (AD), AD falls as a result.

3. Reduced public spending can result in the government expenditure (G) component of AD decreasing too, thus also causing AD to fall, leading to a fall in real GDP to Y_0 to Y_1.

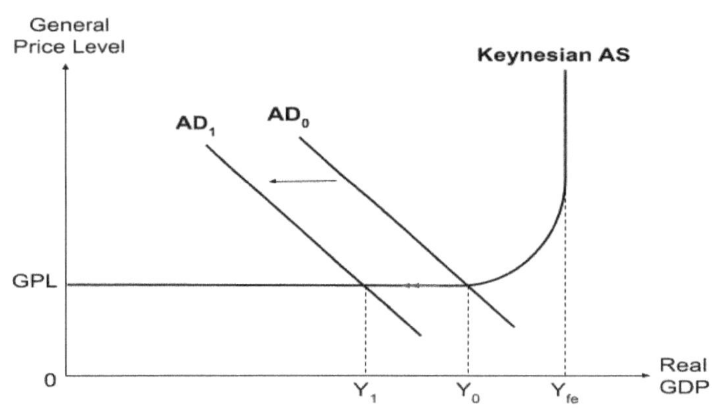

Fig 1: Fall in Economic Growth due to Debt Servicing

4. Increasing taxes and/or reducing public spending to meet debt obligations thus leads to reduced actual economic growth.

Reason 2: Opportunity costs

1. Higher levels of government indebtedness also results in an opportunity cost.

2. As a result of servicing debt repayments and interest costs, when a significant portion of the government's budget is allocated to servicing debt, it leaves less room for productive government expenditures such as infrastructure development, education, healthcare that can stimulate potential economic growth.

3. Such spending would increase the quantity of capital goods in the economy, increase the quality of labour and boost productivity, thus increasing the productive capacity of the economy and the full employment output level.

4. As a result, the high level of government indebtedness hinders potential economic growth and ultimately long-term economic growth.

www.ingramcontent.com/pod-product-compliance
Lightning Source LLC
LaVergne TN
LVHW080659011026
849160LV00014B/1480
* 9 7 8 9 8 1 1 8 9 9 6 6 9 *